CompTIA A+ Practice Test Core 1 (220-1101)

Over 500 practice questions to help you pass the CompTIA A+ Core 1 exam on your first attempt

Ian Neil and Mark Birch

BIRMINGHAM—MUMBAI

CompTIA A+ Practice Test Core 1 (220-1101)

Authors: Ian Neil and Mark Birch

Reviewers: Sahil Kumar and Amir Shetaia

Senior Editor: Ketan Giri

Production Editor: Shantanu Zagade

Editorial Board: Vijin Boricha, Megan Carlisle, Ketan Giri, Alex Mazonowicz, Aaron Nash, Abhishek Rane, and Ankita Thakur

Production reference: 1270923

Published by Packt Publishing Ltd.

Grosvenor House

11 St Paul's Square

Birmingham

B3 1RB

ISBN 978-1-83763-472-9

www.packtpub.com

Contributors

About the Authors

Ian Neil is one of the world's top trainers of Security+. He is able to break down information into manageable chunks so that people with no background knowledge can gain the skills required to become certified. He has recently worked for the US Army in Europe and designed a Security+ course that catered to people from all backgrounds (not just IT professionals), with an extremely successful pass rate. He is an MCT, MCSE, A+, Network+, Security+, CASP, and RESILIA practitioner that has worked with high-end training providers over the past 23 years and was one of the first technical trainers to train Microsoft internal staff when they opened their Bucharest Office in 2006.

Mark Birch is an experienced courseware developer and teacher in both information systems and cyber-security. Mark has been developing content and teaching CompTIA A+ classes for more than 20 years and understands the subject area in great depth. Mark began his career working within the aerospace industry (for a major defense contractor) and has over 30 years' experience consulting, engineering, and deploying secure information systems. He has spent over 20 years working with the United States Military and United Kingdom Armed Forces, helping many students attain their learning goals. Mark has ensured that soldiers, officers, and civilians have had the best opportunities to gain cyber-security accreditation.

About the Reviewers

Sahil Kumar is a software engineer driven by an unwavering passion for innovation and a keen aptitude for problem-solving. With an impressive career spanning eight years, Sahil has honed his expertise in various domains, including IT systems, cybersecurity, endpoint management, and global customer support.

His experience in the tech industry is marked by a commitment to continuous learning and professional growth, as evidenced by his numerous certifications. Sahil holds coveted certifications such as CompTIA A+, CompTIA Security+, ITIL V4, OCI 2023 Foundations Associate, Microsoft SC-200, AZ-900, and a Certificate in Cyber Security (ISC2). This extensive certification portfolio reflects his dedication to staying at the forefront of technology and security trends.

Sahil's proficiency extends beyond the realm of cybersecurity; he is also well-versed in DevSecOps, demonstrating his versatility in tackling multifaceted challenges within the IT landscape. Currently, Sahil is pursuing a master's degree in cybersecurity at New York University, a testament to his commitment to academic excellence and staying at the top of his field. He holds a bachelor's degree in electrical and electronics engineering from Kurukshetra University.

Amir Shetaia is a dedicated professional with a profound passion for embedded systems, robotics, and self-driving vehicles. His career journey is marked by substantial achievements and contributions to the field.

Amir's practical experience includes serving as an Embedded Systems Intern at Valeo, a global automotive technology leader, and successful freelancer on Upwork. He is well-versed in programming languages such as C and Python and possesses expertise with various microcontrollers, including ARM Cortex, PIC, and AVR.

Amir's leadership qualities shine through his role as the Founder and Club Leader of the Mansoura Robotics Club, which has empowered over 1000 students, fostering a deep understanding of robotics fundamentals. He also excels as an Embedded Systems Mentor at CIS Team MU and an Embedded Systems Instructor at UCCD Mansoura Engineering, where he imparts his knowledge and expertise to aspiring engineers.

Amir's impact extends beyond his immediate community, as exemplified by his team's remarkable third prize victory in the Cloud practice exam at the Huawei ICT Competition Global Final. This achievement underscores his unwavering dedication and technical prowess on an international stage.

Amir is a professional who embodies a relentless pursuit of excellence and an unquenchable thirst for knowledge. His commitment to personal and professional growth is evident through his internships at prestigious organizations like Siemens Digital Industries Software, Information Technology Institute (ITI), and Bright Network. These experiences have honed his skills in areas such as Embedded Software Engineering, RTOS, Automotive Protocols, Artificial Intelligence, and more. Amir's journey is a testament to his exceptional grasp of embedded systems and Artificial Intelligence and his passion for sharing knowledge and fostering innovation.

Table of Contents

3

Hardware   43

4

Virtualization and Cloud Computing   67

5

Hardware and Network Troubleshooting   79

Preface

Welcome to the practice test book on CompTIA A+ Core 1 (220-1101), meticulously crafted for those seeking to pass the exam and gain a clear, concise understanding of the foundational concepts, technologies, and practices that underpin modern computer systems.

Who This Book Is For

This A+ practice test book is written for individuals who are preparing to take the CompTIA A+ certification exam. This certification is often sought after by individuals aiming to start or advance their careers in the field of IT and technology support. The book caters to a wide range of individuals, including the following:

- **Aspiring IT professionals**: Those who are new to the IT industry and looking to gain the necessary knowledge and skills to enter the field

- **Entry-level technicians**: Individuals who are already working in IT support roles and wish to validate their skills and knowledge by obtaining the A+ certification

- **Career changers**: People coming from other industries who are interested in transitioning into a career in IT and require a foundational understanding of computer hardware, software, and troubleshooting

- **Students**: Students studying computer science, information technology, or related fields who want to enhance their learning and increase their employability

- **Self-learners**: Individuals who prefer self-paced learning and want to improve their technical skills on their own time, potentially with the aim of changing careers or advancing within their current role

- **IT enthusiasts**: Hobbyists and technology enthusiasts who wish to deepen their knowledge and skills in computer systems and hardware

- **Job seekers**: Those actively seeking employment in IT support or technician roles, as the A+ certification is often a prerequisite or advantage in job applications

- **Military personnel**: Military personnel transitioning to civilian roles in the IT sector, as the A+ certification can aid in their reintegration into the workforce

- **Professional development**: Individuals already in IT roles who are seeking to enhance their skills, stay updated with industry trends, and potentially pursue higher-level certifications in the future

Overall, the CompTIA A+ Core 1 (220-2201) practice test book serves as a valuable resource for anyone looking to prepare for the CompTIA A+ certification exam and establish a solid foundation in IT hardware, software, troubleshooting, and customer service skills.

What This Book Covers

Chapter 1, *Mobile Devices*, prepares you to test your knowledge of all aspects of mobile devices, laptops, tablets, and smartphones, from installation and connectivity to the management of devices.

Chapter 2, *Networking*, helps you test your knowledge of all aspects of networking, including protocols and ports through to different networking devices and the types of connectivity.

Chapter 3, *Hardware*, tests your knowledge of all aspects of hardware, cable types, devices, and the appropriate memory.

Chapter 4, *Virtualization and Cloud Computing*, tests your knowledge of all aspects of virtualization, including client-side virtualization, the use of resources, and security. In addition, it helps you to prepare to work with cloud models and services.

Chapter 5, *Hardware and Network Troubleshooting*, tests your knowledge of the best practices for troubleshooting, then examines how to troubleshoot different aspects of networking and hardware.

Conventions Used

New terms and important words are shown like this: "Cloud computing refers to the provisioning of resources without the need for capital expenditure, in which the **Cloud Service Provider (CSP)** provides all of the hardware and customer lease access."

Get in Touch

Feedback from our readers is always welcome.

General feedback: If you have any questions about this book, please mention the book title in the subject of your message and email us at customercare@packtpub.com.

Errata: Although we have taken every care to ensure the accuracy of our content, mistakes do happen. If you have found a mistake in this book, we would be grateful if you could report this to us. Please visit www.packtpub.com/support/errata and complete the form.

Piracy: If you come across any illegal copies of our works in any form on the Internet, we would be grateful if you could provide us with the location address or website name. Please contact us at copyright@packt.com with a link to the material.

If you are interested in becoming an author: If there is a topic that you have expertise in and you are interested in either writing or contributing to a book, please visit authors.packtpub.com.

Share Your Thoughts

Once you've read *CompTIA A+ Practice Test Core 1 (220-1101)*, we'd love to hear your thoughts! Scan the QR code below to go straight to the Amazon review page for this book and share your feedback.

https://packt.link/r/1837634726

Your review is important to us and the tech community and will help us make sure we're delivering excellent quality content.

How to Use This Book

The purpose of having a practice test book is to facilitate your preparation for the CompTIA A+ Core 1 (220-1101) exam. Prior to attempting a practice test, it's advisable to have either a digital document or a blank sheet of paper at your disposal. While taking the test, it's beneficial to jot down any subjects that are unfamiliar to you or questions you've answered incorrectly. This practice will help pinpoint areas where your understanding is lacking. Following the test, it is recommended that you revisit your study guide to address the identified gaps.

Approach for Navigating Multiple-Choice Queries

Embrace this strategy to effectively tackle multiple-choice queries:

- **Thorough reading**: Immerse yourself in the questions and absorb their nuances
- **Elimination game**: Discard incorrect choices, systematically narrowing your options
- **Refinement process**: Evolve from a 50-50 stance to a 60-40 perspective through a meticulous review
- **Unveil the optimal**: Opt for the finest or most plausible choices when multiple correct answers exist
- **Precision in choice**: Align your selection with the specific query at hand

Exercising Caution in Testing

Avoid these counterproductive actions during your testing endeavor:

- **Overthinking pitfall**: Steer clear of overanalyzing; maintain a balanced mindset
- **Rushing dilemma**: Eschew hasty scanning or racing through the test; maintain a composed pace
- **Doubt's detriment**: Refrain from second-guessing or doubling back; trust your initial instincts
- **Choice constancy**: Resist altering your answers; initial choices often prove sound
- **Comprehensive consistency**: Spare yourself from re-reading the entire test; stay focused on the task at hand

Advice on Additional Resources – Practical Exercise

An additional preparatory resource that could prove valuable is the CompTIA Official Labs. These cloud-based labs offer a practical approach to exam readiness by directly addressing the topics covered in the exam. Particularly beneficial for individuals with minimal or no prior IT experience, these labs serve as excellent tools for gaining hands-on familiarity.

In the context of CompTIA A+ Core 1 (220-1101), a solid grasp of hardware concepts is essential, and the labs effectively facilitate this understanding. A noteworthy aspect is the 12-month access granted, allowing ample time for exploration and learning. Notably, Packt Publishing has secured a substantial discount on the CompTIA official labs and the exam voucher, the details for which are at the back of the book.

What You Will Learn in the CompTIA Official Labs

Once you have paid and signed up for the CompTIA CertMaster Labs for A+ Core 1 (220-1101), you will have access to hands-on practice and skills development using real equipment and software accessed through a remote, browser-based lab environment. Aligned with Official CompTIA courseware and the CompTIA A+ Core 1 (220-1101) exam objectives, CertMaster Labs make it easy for learners to practice and apply their skills in real workplace scenarios in preparation for the certification exam. All lab activities include gradable assessments, offer feedback and hints, and provide a score based on learner inputs, ultimately guiding you to the most correct and efficient path through job tasks.

There are two types of labs in the course:

- **Virtual Workbench Labs** provide learners with valuable hands-on practice installing, configuring, and troubleshooting computer hardware in an immersive 3D environment. Each scenario features a Tutorial Mode to guide the learner through step-by-step instructions, allowing learners to understand and practice 3D controls; an Explore Mode that enables learners to identify and manipulate hardware components in a sandbox environment; and an Assisted Mode that takes learners step by step through a procedure, offering help when needed. This hands-on environment gives learners the ability to learn the tangible aspects of IT and gain real-world experience. Learners can explore how the different components of a desktop, a laptop, and peripherals work together, and will get experience of working through different processes for installing and configuring computer components.

- **Virtual Machine Labs** utilize virtual machines built to simulate a server network so a learner can gain real-world, hands-on experience with tools, applications, and operating systems they would utilize in a job environment, such as Microsoft Windows or Kali Linux. Learners can compare network hardware using the GNS3 network simulator and configure a home router using OpenWRT.

Virtual Machine Labs are also available in different modes:

- **Assisted Labs** guide the learner step by step through tasks, offering assessment and feedback throughout a 10-15 minute experience, allowing the learner to correct any misunderstandings as they proceed through the activity.

- **Applied Labs** present a series of goal-oriented scenarios in a 20-30 minute experience covering multiple topics, scoring the learner's work at the end of the activity based on their ability to successfully complete each scenario. As a result, learners are forced to think critically about how to approach problems without a prescribed set of steps. Currently, Applied Labs are only available for Virtual Machine Lab activities.

The following labs are available:

- Assisted Lab: Exploring the Lab Environment
- Assisted Lab: Installing a Motherboard
- Assisted Lab: Installing Power Supplies
- Assisted Lab: Installing and Configuring System Memory
- Assisted Lab: Installing RAM
- Assisted Lab: Installing CPU and Cooler
- Assisted Lab: Upgrading and Installing GPU and Daisy-Chain Monitors
- Assisted Lab: Exploring the Virtual Machine Lab Environment
- Assisted Lab: Compare Networking Hardware
- Assisted Lab: Compare Wireless Network Technologies
- Assisted Lab: Configure a SOHO Router
- Assisted Lab: Compare Protocols and Ports
- Assisted Lab: Troubleshoot a Network #1
- Assisted Lab: Troubleshoot a Network #2
- APPLIED Lab: Troubleshoot a Network #1
- APPLIED Lab: Troubleshoot a Network #2
- Assisted Lab: Adding Expansion SSD in a Laptop
- Assisted Lab: Upgrading Laptop RAM

- Assisted Lab: Replacing Laptop Non-User Removable Battery

- Assisted Lab: Configuring Laptop Dock and External Peripherals

- Assisted Lab: Deploy a Printer

Accessing the Course Materials

You will receive an access key and registration instructions via email once you have paid and signed up for the CompTIA CertMaster Labs for A+ Core 1 (220-1101).

1

Mobile Devices

Introduction

Mobile devices are in abundance in the workplace, ranging from laptops to tablets and smartphones. It's therefore important that IT technicians have working knowledge of each type of device, including both the storage used and the method of its migration from legacy to modern storage.

Additionally, in your own career, you may have to enable security for smartphones that require you to set up multifactor or biometric authentication, set up cellular communications and mobile hotspots, or connect a corporate user's Bluetooth headset. And, for laptop queries, whether it requires the order of a new device for the engineering department, installation of a new wireless card, or troubleshooting of the display screen, your understanding of laptop hardware, components, and types and size of cards is crucial to ensuring the support you offer is reliable and effective.

In the CompTIA A+ Core 1 (220-1101) exam, Domain 1.0 Mobile Devices is further broken down into the following core objectives:

- 1.1 Given a scenario, install and configure laptop hardware and components
- 1.2 Compare and contrast the display components of mobile devices
- 1.3 Given a scenario, set up and configure accessories and ports of mobile devices
- 1.4 Given a scenario, configure basic mobile-device network connectivity and application support

The rest of this chapter is committed to practice. For each of the concepts defined above, you will be given a series of questions designed to test your knowledge of each core 1 objective as defined by the official certification exam guidance for this domain. Once you have completed these questions and ensured you understand the concepts behind them, you should be fully prepared to do the same in your CompTIA A+ Core 1 (220-1101) exam.

Practice Exam Questions

1.1 Given a scenario, install and configure laptop hardware and components

1. Which of the following is the most secure method to set up a laptop or desktop to use biometric readers?

    A. Set up the laptop/desktop for the person who uses the device

    B. Set up the laptop/desktop so everyone in the accounts department can log in

    C. Allow other departments access to the laptop/desktop

    D. Set up the laptop for user access and allow guest access

2. A hardware engineer is going to upgrade the RAM in a laptop. Before installing the new RAM, which of the following tasks should the hardware engineer complete first?

    A. Purchase a 256 GB DDR3 RAM

    B. Take anti-static precautions by wearing an electrostatic discharge strap

    C. Check the power voltage to the motherboard

    D. Download any operating system updates for the laptop's operating system

3. A user's laptop is working perfectly fine, but for some reason, when they attempt to use it in a coffee shop, it will not power up. The user confirms that the battery is plugged in but notices a small bump on the battery. Which of the following is the most likely cause of this problem?

    A. The power adapter is faulty

    B. The operating system is corrupt

    C. The system fan is not working

    D. The battery has failed, as it is defective and needs replacing

4. What type of RAM would you purchase for a laptop computer?

    A. DIMM

    B. DDR3

    C. SDRAM

    D. SODIMM

5. Which of the following safety precautions do you need to take prior to installing an SSD into a user's laptop? (Choose four)

   A. Clear your desk

   B. Shut down the system

   C. Disconnect the power cable

   D. Remove the battery

   E. Ground yourself by wearing an ESD strap

6. What types of biometric authentication do the iPhone 10 and iPhone 11 use? (Choose two)

   A. Fingerprint

   B. Touch ID

   C. Face ID

   D. Vein

7. A user has put their phone on charging, but the battery is draining quickly and is recharging very slowly. The phone is also hot to the touch. What is wrong with the phone?

   A. The charging cable is faulty

   B. The digitizer is broken

   C. The battery needs to be replaced

   D. The battery is set to low power mode

8. A laptop user tries to surf the internet but finds they have no connectivity. Running the ipconfig /all command produces the following output:

```
IPv4 Address. . . . . . . . . . . : 169.254.10.1
Subnet Mask . . . . . . . . . . . : 255.255.0.0
Default Gateway . . . . . . . . . :
DHCP Enabled                        Yes
```

   Which of the following is the source of this problem?

   A. DNS

   B. DHCP

   C. NETBIOS

   D. Static IP address

9. Which of the following stages do you need to take when migrating a Hard Drive (HDD) to a Solid-State Drive (SSD) in a laptop? (Select all that apply)

    A. Clean the files on your old hard drive and remove redundant data

    B. Connect and initialize the SSD

    C. Make a full backup of your system

    D. Resize the old HDD partition where your data resides to be smaller than the SSD

    E. Clone the old HDD partition

    F. Restore the data onto the SSD

10. A new door access system uses a 13.56-MHz short-band frequency. Which of the following can be used for authentication with this system on a mobile device?

    A. Biometrics

    B. Certificates

    C. OAuth token

    D. NFC

11. A computer technician is going to install a Solid-State Drive (SSD) in a laptop. What is the standard form factor of the drive that the computer technician needs to purchase?

    A. 3.5 inches

    B. 2.5 inches

    C. 5.25 inches

    D. 8 inches

12. John Smith plugged his iPhone into his bedside power socket prior to going to bed, but in the morning, the battery displays a 5% charge. He then goes to breakfast, boils the kettle for a cup of tea, and plugs the phone's charger into the kettle's socket. After 30 minutes, the phone still does not seem to be charging. The phone charger is not approved by Apple. Which of the following steps should he take first to investigate the issue?

    A. Delete unwanted apps

    B. Reset the phone to factory settings

    C. Check the power rating of the charger

    D. Set the battery to low power mode

13. A client wants to connect an external keyboard to an Android tablet. Which of the following connection types are appropriate for this task? (Choose two)

    A. Bluetooth

    B. Ethernet

    C. Lightning cable

    D. USB-C

14. What is the most common use of NFC?

    A. Making contactless payments

    B. Creating a hotspot

    C. Enabling touchscreen

    D. Creating a VPN

1.2 Compare and contrast the display components of mobile devices

1. Which of the following describes the function of a digitizer?

    A. It converts DC power to AC power

    B. It can support a contrast ratio of 2000:1

    C. It controls the brightness setting on an LCD monitor

    D. It is a piece of glass that is installed on a mobile device to enable the touchscreen to function

2. Which of the following is used by a smartphone to change the orientation of the screen?

    A. Bezel

    B. Digitizer

    C. Accelerometer

    D. Gyroscope

3. The external webcam attached to a laptop is switched on, but it is not producing any images. Which of the following can resolve this issue?

    A. Reboot the computer and try again

    B. Purchase a new webcam

    C. Uninstall and then reinstall the webcam software and ensure you have the most up-to-date drivers from the manufacturer's website

    D. Plug the webcam into another USB port

4. What is the purpose of an inverter?

    A. To convert AC to DC power

    B. To enable touchscreen functionality

    C. To convert DC to AC power

    D. To increase readability in low-light conditions

5. When using a high frame rate, the crystals twist or untwist giving the screen a quick response time that helps reduce ghosting and motion trail. Which of the following options is being described?

    A. TN

    B. IPS

    C. VA

    D. CRT

6. You are having trouble with your voice recognition technology on your Windows 10 laptop. Which of the following tasks should you perform first to resolve this issue with minimal effort?

    A. Reboot the laptop

    B. Get an up-to-date driver for the voice recognition software

    C. Enable apps to access your microphone

    D. Purchase an external microphone

7. A user is having trouble reading the screen on their legacy LCD monitor. The screen looks very dim. What do you think is most likely causing the problem?

    A. The brightness has been turned down

    B. The digitizer is broken

    C. The backlight is failing

    D. The VGA cable is damaged

8. A user has a large dark area on their iPhone screen and has taken it to a mobile phone repair shop. The technician looks at the screen and sees that there is no physical damage. What does the technician determine to be the problem?

    A. Water damage

    B. Problem with the inverter

    C. Brightness too low

    D. Broken digitizer

9. Which of the following displays is best for both gaming and graphic design?

    A. LED

    B. LCD

    C. CRT

    D. IPS

10. Which of the following displays is prone to ghosting and can support a contrast ratio of 2000:1?

    A. OLED

    B. VA

    C. IPS

    D. LED

11. What type of screen is used by monitors, tablets, smartphones, and TV screens and does not use a backlight?

    A. CRT

    B. LCD

    C. OLED

    D. LED

12. A user has plugged in two monitors (via a VGA cable and an HDMI cable) and wants to set up dual monitors. However, there does not seem to be an image on the second monitor. What should the user do first to enable dual monitors?

    A. Go to Settings, Home, Display, Multiple Displays, and then select Duplicate these displays

    B. Go to Settings, Home, Projecting to this PC, and then select Extend these displays

    C. Go to Settings, Home, Projecting to this PC, and then select Duplicate these displays

    D. Go to Settings, Home, Display, Multiple Displays, and then select Extend these displays

13. The sales team wants to play a promotional video from an iPhone 10 for the chief executive officer using Bluetooth speakers, but there does not seem to be any sound coming out of the Bluetooth speakers. The sales team has raised a ticket with the IT help desk. What actions should the support technician take to resolve the issue? (Choose two)

    A. Under Settings, enable Bluetooth

    B. Under General, enable Bluetooth

    C. Ensure the phone is within 20 meters of the speakers

    D. Ensure the phone is within 10 meters of the speakers

14. A computer technician is troubleshooting wireless connectivity on a laptop. Where do you think is the most likely location for the wireless antenna?

    A. On the front of the laptop

    B. On the rear of the laptop

    C. On the top of the laptop

    D. Near the fan on the base of the laptop

15. A lawyer left court carrying a large number of case files. They tripped and accidentally dropped some of their files along with their mobile phone that was resting on top. When the lawyer picked up the phone, the screen did not appear broken, but 10 minutes later, when they attempted to send an email from the phone, the mail icon was unresponsive. The same was true for every other app they attempted to access. What do you think happened?

    A. The digitizer broke

    B. There was no power

    C. There were CPU issues

    D. All of the above

16. The touchpad on your laptop is unresponsive. What should you do? (Choose two)

    A. Reboot the laptop

    B. Remove an external mouse that is plugged in

    C. Update the driver

    D. Turn off the gyroscope

1.3 Given a scenario, set up and configure accessories and ports of mobile devices

1. What type of connection does an iPhone 10 charger use?

    A. USB-B

    B. USB-A

    C. USB-C

    D. Lightning

2. A user is trying to plug a USB 3.0 memory stick into their old Windows 7 laptop but is having difficulty doing so. Which of the following could be causing the issue? (Choose two)

    A. The USB 3.0 drive has a different form factor

    B. The USB 3.0 drive is upside down

    C. The laptop does not have a USB 3.0 port

    D. The end of the USB 3.0 drive is damaged

3. What type of connection does a Samsung Galaxy phone use?

    A. USB

    B. USB-C

    C. Micro USB

    D. Mini USB

4. A user is finding it difficult to plug their phone charger into their cell phone, and so orders a new charger from Amazon. However, when the new charger is inserted, the same thing happens. It does not seem to fit. Which of the following is the cause and solution of the issue?

    A. The port that the user is plugging the cable into has a build-up of lint, and they need to use compressed air to clear it

    B. The port that the user is plugging the cable into has a build-up of lint, and they need to blow into the port to clear it

    C. The port that the user is plugging the cable into has a build-up of lint, and they need to spray WD-40 into the port to clear it

    D. The port that the user is plugging the cable into has a build-up of lint, and they need to use a long darning needle to clear it

5. A user goes into a shop and purchases Bluetooth-capable earbuds so that they can listen to music when working out in the gym. However, when they turn on their smartphone and their earbuds, they find they cannot hear the music. What does the user need to do first to resolve this issue? (Choose two)

    A. Install a driver on the phone

    B. Enable Bluetooth

    C. Pair the device

    D. Turn on the music

6. Which of the following types of functionality would a docking station with DisplayPort provide for a laptop user? (Choose three)

    A. Keyboard and mouse

    B. Wi-Fi

    C. Ethernet connectivity

    D. Speakers

    E. Dual-monitor functionality

7. A user is working remotely from home and is due to participate in a Zoom conference call in 15 minutes. Unfortunately, when they boot up their laptop, they find their home wireless network is down. What can the user implement quickly so that they can participate in the conference call? Choose the solution that requires the minimum amount of effort.

    A. Travel 10 miles to the local Starbucks to use their wireless network

    B. Connect the laptop directly to the wireless router using an Ethernet cable

    C. Create a hotspot using a smartphone

    D. Reboot the wireless router

8. A laptop user has been complaining to the help desk that their laptop does not have that many ports. They would like a range of additional ports for a keyboard, a mouse, and a VGA projector. How can the support desk fulfill this request with the least amount of administrative work?

    A. Install a KVM switch

    B. Install a port replicator

    C. Install dual monitors

    D. Install a hub

9. When using a tablet with a touch pen, you get erroneous behavior such as an erratically moving cursor. Which of the following are the first three steps you should take to identify the problem?

    A. Check whether the screen is damaged

    B. Replace the touch pen battery

    C. Recalibrate the touch pen

    D. Clean the touchscreen

10. What type of connection was micro USB replaced by?

    A. Serial

    B. Lightning

    C. USB-C

    D. Parallel

11. What type of connection does an iPhone 14 charger use?

    A. USB-A

    B. USB-B

    C. USB-C

    D. Lightning

12. What type of interface uses a nine-pin RS-232 hardware port?

    A. Parallel

    B. RJ45

    C. RJ11

    D. Serial

13. A user is trying to connect to a Zoom session, but when they select the video option, it fails to open. They then go to the camera app on their desktop to test the webcam, but the webcam also fails to open. The webcam was working the previous day. Which of the following should be done to address this issue? (Choose two)

    A. Ensure that in the camera privacy settings, Allow apps to access this camera is enabled

    B. Unplug the webcam USB cable and try another USB port

    C. Close any other video software applications and turn on the webcam to see whether it will launch

    D. Purchase another webcam as the webcam is broken

14. The touchscreen feature on a Windows 10 computer has stopped working. Which of the following should a technician check?

    A. That there are no air bubbles on the screen

    B. Computer settings

    C. Display settings

    D. Power settings

15. Following an update to the operating system of their desktop computer, the user's webcam is no longer functioning. The user is due to join a Zoom session in 45 minutes time. Which of the following should be their first step to resolve the issue?

    A. Quickly go to the shops and buy another webcam

    B. Reboot their computer

    C. Reinstall the webcam software including any driver updates

    D. Update the operating system

16. A Cornish pasty vendor in Waterloo railway station is having difficulty taking contactless card payments. When the card is tapped, the contactless scanner does not read the card and process the transaction. The customers need to insert their card into the device and enter their pin to make payments. Which of the following technologies is at fault here?

    A. Bluetooth

    B. Wireless

    C. NFC

    D. Infrared

17. A member of the sales team contacts the support desk to say that their cell phone is overheating. Which of the following is causing this to happen? (Choose three)

    A. A cracked screen

    B. Using the phone as a Wi-Fi hotspot

    C. A faulty battery

    D. Using a cheap charging cable

    E. Several outdated applications being left open

18. Which of the following cable types did the Lightning cable replace?

    A. Apple 30-pin connector

    B. Apple 20-pin connector

    C. Apple 25-pin connector

    D. USB-C

1.4 Given a scenario, configure basic mobile-device network connectivity and application support

1. A company issues their sales team smartphones under a CYOD policy. A salesperson decides to watch a film on Netflix when staying at a hotel because it is cheaper than subscribing to the hotel's video packages. After breakfast, they use their smartphone to find directions to the next customer's site, but the internet is not working. What is the most likely reason that the internet is not available?

    A. Network coverage is not available in the area

    B. The phone has a data cap

    C. The Mobile Device Management (MDM) solution pushed out an update that disabled the internet

    D. The company has defaulted on its monthly account payment

2. Which of the following types of authentication is two-factor?

    A. Retina and fingerprint

    B. Password and fingerprint

    C. Password and PIN

    D. Gait and swiping a card

3. A user received a new smartphone through the post and has managed to connect the phone to their wireless network to access the internet. However, when they leave home later that day, all internet access has been lost and they cannot make calls. What has the user forgotten to do when setting up the new phone?

    A. Install the SIM card

    B. Turn on mobile data

    C. Remove the film protecting the screen

    D. Activate Bluetooth

4. A regular gym user has just bought an Apple Watch so that they can monitor their exercise by completing the rings each day. To see their progress in the iPhone app, they will need to pair both devices. What is the easiest method of doing so?

    A. Pair manually using the four-digit Apple Watch passcode

    B. Use the camera on the Apple Watch app on the iPhone

    C. Pair manually using a six-digit passcode

    D. Enter the Apple Watch passcode

5. A mobile salesperson has complained to the service desk that the latest changes to their calendar have appeared on their laptop but have failed to appear on their corporate mobile phone. What should the service desk do to resolve this issue?

    A. Check that the corporate phone battery is above 50%

    B. Reboot the corporate mobile phone

    C. Check that the corporate password has been updated on the calendar application

    D. Remotely wipe the corporate mobile phone

6. What is the benefit of using a Global System for Mobile Communication-based phone?

    A. It can only be used high up a mountain

    B. The Subscriber Identity Card (SIM) is removable and can be inserted into an unlocked handset with the user's chosen provider

    C. It can only be used with a satellite

    D. It can only be used with a WPA3 wireless network

7. In the past year, the sales team from a company has lost eight smartphones containing sensitive company information. Which of the following options would allow the company to remotely wipe any lost smartphone so that commercially sensitive data cannot be compromised?

    A. WPA2 PSK

    B. Disabling Bluetooth

    C. Mobile Device Management (MDM) solution

    D. Using a VPN on all company phones

8. What is the purpose of a Mobile Application Management (MAM) solution? (Choose two)

    A. Patch management

    B. Prevent data transfer to personal apps

    C. Set policies for apps that process corporate data

    D. Remotely wipe devices

9. Where does your Samsung Galaxy back up your data?

    A. Gmail

    B. Google Drive

    C. Knox container

    D. Office 365

10. A user tries to download an app from the Apple App Store onto their iPhone, but the installation fails. What do they need to do next?

    A. Enter their Hotmail account details

    B. Enter their Gmail account details

    C. Enter their iPhone passcode

    D. Enter their Apple ID and password

11. On the 70th anniversary of Edmond Hillary's climb to the summit of Mount Everest, a team from New Zealand plans to follow in his footsteps. Some of the locations that they will visit en route will have very poor connectivity for cell phones. Which of the following would you recommend that they use for communications?

    A. Carrier pigeon

    B. DSL

    C. Hotspot

    D. Satellite

12. A pop star on a worldwide tour has complained to you, their cell phone provider, that their iPhone battery is draining too quickly. They also find when running applications that the weather app is using the most power. What would you recommend they do to prevent battery drain but still allow them to get weather notifications?

    A. Turn off location services

    B. Connect to local wireless networks

    C. Manually enter the locations in the weather app

    D. Change the battery

13. A traveling salesperson was trying to use the GPS on their phone, but it stopped working. They took it to a cell phone store and the support technician took less than one minute to identify the source of the problem and advised the salesperson to change the battery. How did the technician resolve the issue?

    A. Turned on Bluetooth

    B. Turned off power conservation mode

    C. Cleaned the touchscreen

    D. Turned on Wi-Fi

14. A foreign government intends to track an intelligence agent's phone at all times while they travel abroad. Which of the following can prevent them from doing so?

    A. Set location services to pause

    B. Keep the device in a laptop bag

    C. Turn off location services

    D. Delete location services

15. Where does your iPhone back your files up to?

    A. Boot Camp

    B. Office 365

    C. Google Drive

    D. iCloud

16. How can you verify that Bluetooth is enabled on a Windows 10 phone?

    A. The Bluetooth tile is blue

    B. The Bluetooth tile is white

    C. The Bluetooth tile is green

    D. The Bluetooth tile is gray

17. What can you use to prevent PII and sensitive data from being shared outside the company over corporate email?

    A. Legal hold

    B. MailTips

    C. Firewall

    D. DLP

18. Comparing Global System for Mobile Communication (GSM)-based phones and Code Division Multiple Access (CDMA)-based handsets, which of the following statements is true?

    A. Both GSM and CDMA phones have removable SIM cards

    B. Neither GSM nor CDMA phones have removable SIM cards

    C. GSM phones have removable SIM cards, while CDMA phones have no SIM cards

    D. CDMA phones have removable SIM cards, while GSM phones have no SIM cards

19. A mobile salesperson has been asked to cover a different territory for a three-month period. On their first day working in the new territory, their smartphone cannot access the internet nor make any calls. Which of the following needs to be carried out so that the salesperson can use their smartphone?

    A.   Firmware update

    B.   PRL update

    C.   Turn on location services

    D.   Restart the smartphone

20. A user's smartphone is unable to make a 4G connection. What should they do to resolve this issue?

    A.   Go to Settings, then Mobile Data, and enable Wi-Fi calling

    B.   Go to Wi-Fi, then Mobile Data, and enable mobile data

    C.   Go to Settings, then Mobile Data, and enable mobile data

    D.   Go to Wi-Fi, then enable Wi-Fi calling

21. Which of the following are true about Google Workspace? (Select all that apply)

    A.   It is a subscription service with a 14-day free trial

    B.   You can create virtual machines

    C.   You can conduct video meetings

    D.   You can access Google Drive

    E.   There is at least 30 GB of storage per user

    F.   You need a live.com email to access it

22. The FBI informs a business that one of their employees might be carrying out some criminal activities. They want to ensure that any messages sent via corporate email are retained and not deleted as these emails might be needed as evidence for the case against the employee. Which of the following solutions will the system administrator implement?

    A.   Back up the employee's mailbox

    B.   Apply a legal hold

    C.   Set up a forensic toolkit

    D.   Maintain the chain of custody

23. Which of the following are valid ways to test a Bluetooth connection? (Choose three)

   A. If you have earbuds, verify that the Bluetooth connect tile is blue

   B. If you are wearing a headset, go into Zoom (or some other video calling service), then locate Audio Settings, Speaker, and select Test speaker

   C. If you have earbuds, try playing music on your phone

   D. If you are wearing a headset, go into Zoom (or some other video calling service), then locate Audio Settings, Microphone, and select Test mic

   E. If you are wearing a headset, go into Zoom (or some other video calling service), then locate Video Settings, Speaker, and select Test speaker

   F. If you are wearing a headset, go into Zoom (or some other video calling service), then locate Video Settings, Microphone, and select Test mic

2

Networking

Introduction

Modern technology is increasingly characterized by the interconnectivity of our devices. This means that to keep pace with this progress and provide consistent and effective support, it is imperative that IT professionals have a working knowledge of networking concepts ranging from IP addresses to the different types of wireless networks.

You will need to know what ports different applications use in order to open those ports on the firewall and allow them to communicate. IT administrators also need to know how to troubleshoot issues when users cannot connect to the network, whether the source of the problem is a DNS or IP error. Wireless networks are a common part of everyday life, and it is vital that you have the knowledge and experience to determine which type of wireless network is best for a given scenario. The practice test in this chapter will test the application of the information that you have gained from previous study.

In the CompTIA A+ Core 1 (220-1101) certification examination, Domain 2.0 Networking makes up 20% of the assessment and is therefore a vital component of a student's successful preparation. This domain is further broken down into the following core objectives:

- 2.1 Compare and contrast Transmission Control Protocol (TCP) and User Datagram Protocol (UDP) ports, protocols, and their purposes

- 2.2 Compare and contrast common networking hardware

- 2.3 Compare and contrast protocols for wireless networking

- 2.4 Summarize services provided by networked hosts

- 2.5 Given a scenario, install and configure basic wired/wireless small office/home office (SOHO) networks

- 2.6 Compare and contrast common network configuration concepts

- 2.7 Compare and contrast internet connection types, network types, and their features

- 2.8 Given a scenario, use networking tools

The rest of this chapter is committed to practice. For each of the concepts defined above, you will be given a series of questions designed to test your knowledge of each core 1 objective as defined by the official certification exam guidance for this domain. Once you have completed these questions and ensured you understand the concepts behind them, you should be fully prepared to do the same on your CompTIA A+ Core 1 (220-1101) exam.

Practice Exam Questions

2.1 Compare and contrast TCP and UDP ports, protocols, and their purposes

1. A systems administrator needs to use a protocol for secure remote access to network devices. Which of the following should they use?

    A. Telnet TCP port 23

    B. SSH TCP port 22

    C. RDP TCP port 3389

    D. SNMP UDP port 161

2. When an online store alerts you that you are being redirected to a secure server, what protocol should be seen in the URL?

    A. TFTP

    B. HTTPS

    C. HTTP

    D. SSH

3. Which of the following mail clients downloads the email, stores it on the local computer, and does not retain a copy on the mail server?

    A. POP

    B. IMAP

    C. SMTP

    D. SSH

4. Which application protocol is used in Windows operating systems for file and print sharing?

    A. 137-139

    B. 67/68

    C. 445

    D. 389

5. Which of the following standard ports is used by secure Post Office Protocol (POP)?

    A. 110

    B. 995

    C. 993

    D. 143

6. Which of the following protocols is connectionless and used for streaming video or audio?

    A. TCP

    B. RDP

    C. UDP

    D. TFTP

7. Which of the following ports is used by the secure version of the protocol that can provide statuses and reports of all network devices?

    A. 161

    B. 389

    C. 110

    D. 162

8. Which of the following protocols uses TCP ports 20/21 and transfers data in cleartext?

    A. TFTP

    B. FTP

    C. SSH

    D. FTPS

9. Which of the following are default ports for HTTP and HTTPS traffic? (Choose two)

    A. 23

    B. 80

    C. 110

    D. 443

    E. 445

10. TCP is connection-orientated and uses a three-way handshake. What is the correct sequence
    of the handshake?

    A. SYN, ACK, and SYN-ACK

    B. SIGNAL, CONNECT, ACKNOWLEDGE

    C. SYN-ACK, ACK, and SYN

    D. SYN, SYN-ACK, and ACK

11. A system administrator is setting up a new firewall and needs to allow SMTP traffic to flow
    through. Which of the following TCP ports must be enabled for inbound traffic?

    A. 21

    B. 22

    C. 23

    D. 25

12. Which of the following standard ports is used by secure IMAP?

    A. 993

    B. 110

    C. 995

    D. 143

13. Which of the following is an unsecure remote access protocol that can have its password stolen
    by a protocol analyzer?

    A. SSL

    B. SSH

    C. Telnet

    D. RDP

2.2 Compare and contrast common networking hardware

QTYPE: MCQ-MULTI_ANSWER

1. A junior network administrator has been asked to identify the front and back of a patch panel. Which of the following is true? (Choose two)

    A. The front of the patch panel is where cabling running through the company terminates at the insulation displacement connector (IDC)

    B. The back of the patch panel is where cabling running through the company terminates at the insulation displacement connector (IDC)

    C. The front of the patch panel has prewired RJ45 ports

    D. The back of the patch panel has prewired RJ45 ports

2. Cloud Service Providers (CSP) need to be able to rapidly provision servers and networks using scripting. What type of networking provides this?

    A. Wide area network (WAN)

    B. Local area network (LAN)

    C. Software-defined networking (SDN)

    D. Storage area network (SAN)

3. What type of firewall can perform URL filtering, content filtering, and malware inspection?

    A. Stateless firewall

    B. Host-based firewall

    C. Stateful firewall

    D. Unified Threat Management (UTM)

4. What is the purpose of an Optical Network Terminal (ONT) installed at a customer's home?

    A. It provides fiber to the curb (FTTC)

    B. The ONT converts optical signals to electrical signals

    C. The ONT converts electrical signals and converts them to optical signals

    D. The ONT is located in a street cabinet

5. Which of the following allows a host to pull power for a device through an ethernet cable plugged into a switch?

   A. POE

   B. Thunderbolt

   C. Managed switch

   D. Shielded twisted pair

6. Which of the following network devices is used to reduce the size of broadcast domains in a LAN?

   A. Load balancer

   B. Managed switch

   C. Router

   D. Hub

7. Which of the following technologies allows virtual servers to connect to high-speed storage?

   A. SAN

   B. PAN

   C. Cluster

   D. RAID 0

8. A company wants to use POE as powering switches is more efficient than using an AC adapter and will help reduce the electricity bill. However, two of the switches do not support POE. Bearing in mind that cost is a concern, what can the network engineer do to solve this issue?

   A. Purchase an uninterruptible power supply (UPS)

   B. Purchase a generator

   C. Install power injectors

   D. Purchase two POE capable switches

9. What type of switch is unpacked from the box, turned on, has either 4 or 8 ports, and is used in very small networks?

   A. Managed switch

   B. Aggregate switch

   C. Power diode switch

   D. Unmanaged switch

10. Which of the following legacy network hardware devices sends any incoming packets it receives to all ports connected to the device?

    A. Load balancer

    B. Switch

    C. Router

    D. Hub

11. If a network-based firewall is set up to allow HTTP and HTTPS traffic, what happens when a user tries to download a document using FTP?

    A. Document will be downloaded

    B. Document will be blocked by its host-based firewall

    C. Implicit deny

    D. Explicit deny

12. Which of the following statements about cable modems are true? (Select all that apply)

    A. A cable modem is similar to a DSL router but uses coax

    B. A cable modem is connected to the local router via an RJ45 port

    C. A cable modem accesses the provider's network via a short segment of coax

    D. The coax used by a cable modem is terminated using threaded F-type connectors

13. What are the THREE layers of an SDN?

    A. Application layer

    B. Transport layer

    C. Control layer

    D. Infrastructure layer

    E. Data link layer

    F. Physical layer

14. Which of the following is true concerning a network interface card used with a Cat 5 cable?

    A. The NIC card will use a BNC connector

    B. The NIC card will use an RJ45 connector

    C. The NIC card will use an RJ11 connector

    D. The NIC card will run at a speed of 10Mbps

15. What version of Power over Ethernet (POE) can draw power up to 25W?

    A. 802.11

    B. 802.3at

    C. 802.3bt

    D. 802.3af

16. Which of the following are true about different types of DSL? Select TWO.

    A. ADSL provides the same upload and download speeds

    B. ADSL provides a fast download but a slow upload speed

    C. The symmetric version of DSL provides a fast upload and a slow download speed

    D. The symmetric version of DSL provides the same upload and download speed

2.3 Compare and contrast protocols for wireless networking

1. Which of the following bands work with radios that are single-band 2.4GHz? (Select all that apply)

    A. Wi-Fi 6

    B. Wi-Fi 5

    C. 802.11g

    D. 802.11b

    E. Wi-Fi 4

2. Which of the following wireless frequencies supports both 5GHz and 2.4GHz?

    A. 802.11b

    B. 802.11g

    C. 802.11a

    D. 802.11ax

3. A user is trying and failing to get their Bluetooth earbuds to connect to their smartphone to listen to music. Which of the following actions should the user carry out? Select TWO.

    A. Pair the device

    B. Go to Settings | Wi-Fi, then enable Bluetooth

    C. Go to Settings | Mobile Data, then enable Bluetooth

    D. Go to Settings, then enable Bluetooth

4. Which of the following can be used as a bridge to connect two wireless networks over a distance of 25 miles?

    A. GPS

    B. Long-range fixed wireless

    C. Unlicensed wireless

    D. Licensed wireless

5. Which of the following wireless protocols can be used for contactless payments?

    A. Bluetooth

    B. RFID

    C. NFC

    D. Tethering

6. Which of the following standards supports only the 5GHz frequency band?

    A. 802.11a

    B. 802.11b

    C. 802.11g

    D. 802.11n

7. Which of the following statements about 2.4GHz wireless frequency is true? (Choose two)

    A. 2.4GHz is slower than 5GHz

    B. 2.4GHz is faster than 5GHz

    C. 2.4GHz covers a greater distance than 5GHz

    D. 2.4GHz covers a smaller distance than 5GHz

8. Which of the following wireless technologies has the fastest throughput?

    A. 802.11ac

    B. 802.11ax

    C. 802.11a

    D. 802.11b

9. Which of the following wireless standards are backward-compatible with 802.11g?

    A. 802.11b

    B. 802.11a

    C. 802.11n

    D. 801.11ac

10. Which of the following statements about the 5GHz wireless frequency are true? (Choose two)

    A. 5GHz is more effective at propagating through solid surfaces than 2.4GHz

    B. 5GHz is less effective at propagating through solid surfaces than 2.4GHz

    C. 5GHz supports more individual channels and suffers less congestion than 2.4GHz

    D. 5GHz supports more individual channels and suffers more congestion than 2.4GHz

11. Which of the following standards supports MIMO technology?

    A. 802.11a

    B. 802.11b

    C. 802.11g

    D. 802.11n

2.4 Summarize services provided by networked hosts

1. The helpdesk has been overwhelmed by network users saying that they cannot access any network resources. What server should the helpdesk ensure is up and running?

    A. Domain controller

    B. DNS server

    C. DHCP server

    D. Mail server

2. If a home user has an internet connection but cannot connect to any websites and reports this to their ISP, what should the system administrator of the ISP check first?

    A. The user's login credentials

    B. The IP address of the user's device

    C. The destination web servers

    D. The DNS server settings

3. What type of server can provide webpage caching?

    A. File server

    B. Proxy server

    C. UTM firewall

    D. Web server

4. What type of network is used in oil or gas refineries?

    A. Production network

    B. Local area network

    C. SCADA network

    D. MAN

5. Which of the following could be considered Internet of Things? (Choose two)

    A. Alexa

    B. Alarm clock

    C. Smart meter

    D. Headset

6. Which of the following is true about spam gateways? (Select all that apply)

    A. They use SPF, DKIM, and DMARC to verify the authenticity of the mail servers sending emails

    B. They are used to send out spam to other organizations

    C. They use a DLP system to stop PII and other sensitive information from leaving your network

    D. They filter out incoming messages to prevent them from being delivered to users' mailboxes

7. An organization has installed 20 web servers into an existing web array of 30 web servers. How can this array of web servers be optimized for faster response times?

    A. Set up a cluster

    B. Install a load balancer

    C. Install a proxy server

    D. Install a DNS server

8. What type of server uses port 25?

    A. DNS server

    B. DHCP server

    C. Proxy server

    D. Mail server

9. What type of content is hosted on a web server?

    A. Stored files

    B. Websites that contain home folders

    C. Mailboxes

    D. Authentication, authorization, and accounting information

10. A user has a mapped drive that shows a UNC path of \\server1\data. Which of the following network services are they accessing?

    A. Print server

    B. File share

    C. Syslog

    D. Proxy server

11. Which of the following can authenticate a supplicant without holding a copy of the relevant directory services?

    A. Syslog server

    B. DNS server

    C. Proxy server

    D. RADIUS server

12. A system administrator has installed a new laser printer for the customer service team. After installation, they attempt to print a test page, but it fails to print. What should they do first?

    A. Calibrate the printer

    B. Reboot the printer

    C. Download the driver from the manufacturer's website

    D. Change the toner cartridge

13. Which of the following servers centralizes log files from multiple servers?

   A. Syslog

   B. DHCP

   C. File server

   D. Domain controller

14. What is the first thing a home user should do when they purchase an IoT device such as a baby monitor?

   A. Update the device

   B. Disconnect the internet

   C. Read the user manual

   D. Reset the default password

2.5 Given a scenario, install and configure basic wired/wireless small office/home office (SOHO) networks

1. What type of IP address should a server be given?

   A. Dynamic

   B. Static

   C. Automatic Private Internet Protocol Addressing (APIPA)

   D. Public

2. What is the limitation of using a private IPv4 address?

   A. It can only be used internally

   B. It can only be used for networks of up to 1,000 hosts

   C. It does not have a network ID

   D. It does not have a host ID

3. A systems administrator is configuring an IP address on the external port of the firewall that connects to the WAN. Which of the following IP addresses will they use?

   A. 131.107.1.1

   B. 192.168.1.1

   C. 169.254.1.223

   D. 172.16.5.13

   E. 10.10.15.6

4. Which of the following is the default subnet mask for a Class B IPv4 address?

    A. 255.0.0.0

    B. 255.255.0.0

    C. 255.255.255.0

    D. 169.254.1.1

5. If you work from home and need to connect to the internet, which of the following devices are you most likely to use?

    A. Hub

    B. Router

    C. Switch

    D. WAP

6. Which of the following is a valid IPv4 address?

    A. 10.1.1.0

    B. 255.255.255.128

    C. 212.15.1.2

    D. 12.1.1.255

7. A Windows server has been configured with both IPv4 and IPv6 addresses. What is this known as?

    A. Double stack

    B. Double IP addressing

    C. Dual IP addressing

    D. Dual stack

8. Which of the following is the reason why a desktop might be allocated an IP address of 169.254.11.2? (Select all that apply)

    A. The desktop might have a bad cable or cannot send its broadcast to the DHCP server

    B. The desktop might not be able to contact a DNS server

    C. The desktop might not be able to connect to a domain controller

    D. The desktop might have been allocated a duplicate IP address

9. A user is unable to access the internet, and when the system administrator runs the ipconfig/all command, they get the following output:

```
IPv4 Address. . . . . . . . . . . : 132.24.0.1
Subnet Mask . . . . . . . . . . . : 255.255.0.0
Default Gateway . . . . . . . . . :
```

Which of the following is the source of this problem?

A. DNS

B. Gateway

C. Private IPv4 address

D. Dynamic IP address

10. How many bits does an IPv4 address use?

A. 32

B. 8

C. 16

D. 64

11. Which of the following is an IPv6 address?

A. 10.1.1.1

B. B4-2E-99-C0-75-45

C. 169.254.1.5

D. 2001:0dC8:0000:0000:0abc:0000:def0:2311

12. An installation engineer has installed a new router in a SOHO network that consists of five users. During testing, they noticed that all devices have APIPAs. Printers and file shares are still working, but the hosts cannot access the internet. Which of the following has the installation engineer MOST LIKELY forgotten to configure on the router?

A. NETBIOS

B. SMTP

C. DNS

D. SMB

13. How can you shorten the following IPv6 address:
    2001:0dC8:0000:0000:0abc:0000:def0:2311?

    A. 2001:0dC8::0abc::def0:2311

    B. 2001:0dC8::0000:0abc:0000:def0:2311

    C. 2001:dC8::abc::def:2311

    D. 2001:dC8::abc:0:def0:2311

14. Which of the following is a public IPv4 address?

    A. 10.10.10.1

    B. 172.16.1.3

    C. 126.1.1.1

    D. 192.168.5.6

15. How many bits does an IPv6 address use?

    A. 16

    B. 32

    C. 64

    D. 128

2.6 Compare and contrast common network configuration concepts

1. The financial director of an enterprise raised a ticket as they were unable to connect to any network resources. What should the system administrator check first?

    A. DHCP server

    B. SNMP

    C. RADIUS server

    D. DNS server

2. What DNS record needs to be allocated to a host with an IP address of 2001:0436:2CA1:0057:0023:0567:5673:0005?

    A. A

    B. AAA

    C. MX

    D. TXT

3. What is the default lease duration of a Microsoft DHCP server?

   A. 12 days

   B. 14 days

   C. 8 days

   D. 2 days

4. Users in a small company cannot access the mail server on Monday morning. The system administrator had migrated the old mail server to a new version but did not update the DNS record for the mail server. What DNS records do they need to update?

   A. MX

   B. A

   C. AAA

   D. SRV

5. What type of network would be a single site with all users in close proximity, secure, and connected by one or more switches?

   A. WAN

   B. MAN

   C. LAN

   D. CAN

6. Which of the following uses cryptography to confirm that the source server that an email came from was legitimate?

   A. SPF

   B. DMARC

   C. Syslog

   D. DKIM

7. One of the users in a company keeps raising support tickets for very minor issues. The IT team wants to be able to track him by his IP address. The company is using a DHCP server to dynamically allocate IP addresses. How can the IT team set this user up so that he gets the same IP address from the DHCP server?

   A. Create a new scope for him

   B. Create a customized lease duration for him

   C. Create a static IP address for him

   D. Create a reservation for him

8. Which of the following technologies allows multiple networks to be created within a switch?

   A. VLAN

   B. Proxy Server

   C. Firewall

   D. Router

9. The spam gateway was fooled by spam coming from many different fake domains. Which of the following can be implemented to prevent these emails from accessing the company network?

   A. Firewall

   B. Content filter

   C. DMARC

   D. Proxy server

10. A network administrator is planning to divide the company's network into three subnets. What do they need to configure in the DHCP server so that each subnet gets a certain range of IP addresses that are unique to that subnet?

    A. Scope

    B. Reservation

    C. Lease

    D. Superscope

11. What is the DNS record used by a host with an IP address of 131.122.14.12?

    A. A

    B. AAA

    C. MX

    D. SPF

12. What is the sequence of the DHCP handshake?

    A. ACK, OFFER, REQUEST, DISCOVER

    B. DISCOVER, OFFER, REQUEST, ACK

    C. DISCOVER, REQUEST, OFFER, ACK

    D. REQUEST, OFFER, DISCOVER, ACK

13. Which of the following is a method that can be used to securely connect a remote user's laptop to a corporate server from overseas?

    A. WAN

    B. SSL

    C. DHCP

    D. VPN

14. Which of the following tools can be used to prevent spear phishing or spam attacks? (Select all that apply)

    A. Stateless firewall

    B. SPF

    C. DKIM

    D. DMARC

2.7 Compare and contrast internet connection types, network types, and their features

1. What type of network is the internet an example of?

    A. MAN

    B. PAN

    C. WAN

    D. LAN

2. A mountaineering team is going to climb Mount Everest for charity. However, once they are 1,000 meters above the base camp, they find that they cannot use their cellular phones to communicate with the admin team back in the base camp. How can they climb the mountain and still communicate with the base camp?

    A. Cable modem

    B. Satellite

    C. GPS

    D. Wireless

3. An organization using unshielded twisted pair cabling has been suffering from Electromagnetic Interference (EMI). What can the organization implement to protect from EMI and also provide high-speed communication at the same time?

    A. Fiber

    B. Coax

    C. STP

    D. 10-BASE T

4. What is the main type of connection used by an iPhone 11?

    A. DSL

    B. Wireless

    C. Cellular

    D. Satellite

5. Which of the following statements are true about a Wireless Internet Service Provider (WISP)? (Choose two)

   A. They manufacture the most modem wireless access points

   B. They install long-range fixed-access wireless technology

   C. They provide a bridge between the customer and their service provider networks

   D. They monitor the wireless bandwidth for corporate customers

6. Which of the following best describes a WAN?

   A. An unsecure network over a very large geographical area

   B. A secure fast network with all users in close proximity

   C. A boundary network that protects the LAN

   D. All of the above

7. Which of the following technologies would allow a network host to be allocated an IP address based on its MAC address?

   A. SMTP

   B. DHCP

   C. SSL

   D. DNS

8. A small solicitor's firm has just moved into a listed building. They are not allowed to drill into the walls and have paid a contractor to install a wireless router that connects all of the devices to the wireless network, meaning they do not need physical cables. What type of network has the contractor implemented?

   A. LAN

   B. PAN

   C. WLAN

   D. WAN

9. A company's telephone line has failed due to adverse weather, and their internet connection has been subsequently lost. What type of internet access must they be using for this to occur?

   A. DSL

   B. Satellite

   C. Fiber

   D. Cable modem

2.8 Given a scenario, use networking tools

1. Which of the following tools can be used to test a network card or switch port?

   A. Crimping tool

   B. Cable stripper

   C. Punch-down tool

   D. Loopback plug

2. Which of the following tools will be used by a network administrator to score the cable jacket and remove it from the cable so that it can be attached to an RJ45 plug?

   A. Crimper

   B. Pliers

   C. Cable stripper

   D. Loopback plug

3. What type of tool would be used to terminate wires into an IDC block?

   A. Punch-down tool

   B. Crimping tool

   C. Cable stripper

   D. Cable tester

4. The CEO of a company is unable to obtain a network connection. The ports on the patch panel are not labeled. Which network tool will the system administrator use to identify the port that the CEO is using?

   A. Crimping tool

   B. Punch-down tool

   C. Optical Time Domain Reflectometer (OTDR)

   D. Toner probe

5. Which of the following is the cheapest solution to monitor outbound traffic in an Ethernet network?

   A. Network tap

   B. Loopback plug

   C. Spectrum analyzer

   D. Toner probe

6. A network engineer found that the RJ45 connection on an Ethernet cable had come loose and wanted to replace the RJ45 plug. Which of the following tools would they use to carry out this task?

    A. Punch-down tool

    B. Cable stripper

    C. Crimping tool

    D. Pliers

7. A system administrator has a problem with their wireless access point. To troubleshoot the problem and measure the signal strength, what tool should they use?

    A. Wi-Fi analyzer

    B. Protocol analyzer

    C. Bandwidth monitor

    D. Radio frequency interference

8. What tool should a network administrator use to measure whether a cable in a wall socket has a permanent connection to a patch panel?

    A. Loopback plug

    B. Cable tester

    C. A bandwidth monitor

    D. OTDR

3

Hardware

Introduction

In the vast realm of information technology, hardware serves as the solid foundation upon which the digital world thrives. From the tiniest microchip to the largest server, hardware is the tangible infrastructure that powers our digital existence. Understanding its intricacies is not only crucial for aspiring IT professionals but also essential for anyone seeking to navigate the digital landscape effectively.

In the CompTIA A+ Core 1 (220-1101) certification examination, Domain 3.0 Hardware makes up 25% of the assessment and is therefore a pivotal section. It is evident that mastering the principles of hardware is of paramount importance for success in this certification. This domain is further broken down into the following core objectives:

- 3.1 Explain basic cable types and their connectors, features, and purposes

- 3.2 Install the appropriate RAM given a scenario

- 3.3 Select and install storage devices given a scenario

- 3.4 Install and configure motherboards, CPUs, and add-on cards given a scenario

- 3.5 Install or replace the appropriate power supply given a scenario

- 3.6 Deploy and configure multifunction devices/printers and settings given a scenario

- 3.7 Install and replace printer consumables given a scenario

The rest of this chapter is committed to practice. For each of the concepts defined above, you will be given a series of questions designed to test your knowledge of each core 1 objective as defined by the official certification exam guidance for this domain. Once you have completed these questions and ensured you understand the concepts behind them, you should be fully prepared to do the same on your CompTIA A+ Core 1 (220-1101) exam.

Practice Exam Questions

3.1 Explain basic cable types and their connectors, features, and purposes

1. What is the main limitation of using copper cables for high-speed data transmission?

    A. Signal attenuation

    B. Interference from electromagnetic fields

    C. Limited bandwidth

    D. Insufficient insulation

2. Which tool is commonly used to troubleshoot a fiber optic cable?

    A. Optical Time Domain Reflectometer (OTDR)

    B. Wire cutter

    C. Ethernet cable tester

    D. Multimeter

3. When would you use an ST connector in networking and what is a key benefit?

    A. Single-mode fiber

    B. Multi-mode fiber

    C. High-density networks

    D. Coaxial cables

4. What is the maximum distance limitation of Cat 5 cables for Ethernet networking?

    A. 100 meters

    B. 150 meters

    C. 200 meters

    D. 250 meters

5. Which of the following tools is commonly used to add lines to the demarcation point (demarc)?

    A. Punch-down tool

    B. Wire stripper

    C. Cable tester

    D. Crimping tool

6. In which of the following scenarios would you use an RJ11 connector?

   A. Connecting a telephone handset to a wall jack

   B. Connecting a computer to a router

   C. Connecting a printer

   D. Connecting a TV to a cable box

7. When using a Gigabit network card, what is the maximum data transmission speed limitation of Cat 5 cables?

   A. 100 Mbps

   B. 1 Gbps

   C. 10 Gbps

   D. 40 Gbps

8. Which operating system commonly utilizes Thunderbolt cables for high-speed data transfer and device connectivity?

   A. macOS

   B. Windows

   C. Linux

   D. Android

9. What tool is commonly used to create an RJ45 cable?

   A. Crimping tool

   B. Wire stripper

   C. Punch-down tool

   D. Multimeter

10. In which scenario would you commonly use a Lightning to USB cable?

   A. Charging an iPhone

   B. Connecting a printer to a computer

   C. Transferring data between two computers

   D. Connecting a monitor to a laptop

11. What type of cable has a T568B connection on one end and a T568A connection on the other end?

   A. Crossover cable

   B. Straight-through cable

   C. Coaxial cable

   D. Fiber optic cable

12. What is the actual speed difference between USB and USB 2?

   A. USB offers a speed of 12 Mbps, while USB 2 offers a speed of 480 Mbps

   B. USB and USB 2 have the same speed of 480 Mbps

   C. USB 2 offers a speed of 12 Mbps, while USB offers a speed of 480 Mbps

   D. USB and USB 2 have variable speeds depending on the version

13. When should plenum-grade cables be used in networking installations?

   A. Air-handling spaces

   B. Outdoor environments

   C. High-speed data transfer

   D. Long-distance connectivity

14. When would you use Shielded Twisted Pair (STP) cables in networking installations?

   A. High electromagnetic interference (EMI) environments

   B. Outdoor installations

   C. Long-distance connections

   D. Low electromagnetic interference (EMI) environments

15. When are F-type connectors commonly used in networking?

   A. Ethernet network connections

   B. Fiber optic network connections

   C. Cable television (CATV) connections

   D. Wi-Fi network connections

16. A junior IT technician has inadvertently cut the end of an Ethernet cable with a sharp knife. What three tools do you need to repair it?

    A. Wire cutters, a crimping tool, and an RJ45 connector

    B. Screwdriver, electrical tape, and an RJ45 connector

    C. Soldering iron, heat shrink tubing, and an RJ45 connector

    D. Pliers, a multimeter, and an RJ45 connector

17. You are setting up a fiber optic network and need to choose between SC and LC connectors. Which connector type provides a higher density and is commonly used in data centers?

    A. SC connector

    B. LC connector

    C. ST connector

    D. FC connector

18. Which of the following interfaces is commonly used to connect external storage devices to a computer at high speeds?

    A. USB 2.0

    B. HDMI

    C. eSATA

    D. VGA

19. Which of the following is a primary advantage of using DisplayPort as a video interface?

    A. Simultaneous video and audio transmission

    B. Compatibility with older display devices

    C. Support for 4K and higher resolutions

    D. Lower cost compared to other interfaces

3.2 Install the appropriate RAM given a scenario

1. What is the primary purpose of virtual RAM (or virtual memory) in a computer system?

    A. To provide additional storage space for files and documents

    B. To improve system performance by extending available memory

    C. To create a backup of the system's physical RAM

    D. To facilitate faster data transfer between the CPU and GPU

2. What is the primary reason for using DDR (Double Data Rate) RAM in computer systems?

    A. Improved data transfer rates

    B. Increased storage capacity

    C. Enhanced power efficiency

    D. Reduced latency

3. Which type of memory module is commonly used in laptops and small form factor computers?

    A. DIMM RAM

    B. RIMM RAM

    C. MicroDIMM RAM

    D. SODIMM RAM

4. What is the primary purpose of ECC (Error-Correcting Code) RAM in a computer system?

    A. To provide faster data transfer between the CPU and RAM

    B. To enhance graphics processing capabilities

    C. To detect and correct memory errors

    D. To increase the storage capacity of the RAM

5. What is the primary benefit of using a dual-channel RAM configuration, which utilizes two differently colored memory slots, in a computer system?

    A. Increased storage capacity

    B. Faster data transfer rates

    C. Improved graphics performance

    D. Lower power consumption

6. What is the primary advantage of using a quad-channel RAM configuration in a computer system?

    A. Increased storage capacity

    B. Enhanced multitasking capabilities

    C. Improved data transfer rates

    D. Lower latency in memory access

7. DDR RAM is a type of computer memory that offers improved data transfer rates compared to earlier memory technologies. Which of the following options correctly matches the lowest speed for each version of DDR RAM?

    A. DDR2 – 400 MHz, DDR3 – 800 MHz, DDR4 – 2,133 MHz

    B. DDR2 – 800 MHz, DDR3 – 1,600 MHz, DDR4 – 3,200 MHz

    C. DDR2 – 1,333 MHz, DDR3 – 1,866 MHz, DDR4 – 2,400 MHz

    D. DDR2 – 2,000 MHz, DDR3 – 2,400 MHz, DDR4 – 3,200 MHz

8. Which of the following options would be the best choice for a gaming PC in terms of disk, CPU, and RAM?

    A. HDD, AMD Ryzen 3, 8 GB DDR3

    B. SSD, Intel Core i5, 8 GB DDR4

    C. HDD, Intel Core i9, 32 GB DDR3

    D. SSD, Intel Core i7, 16 GB DDR4

3.3 Given a scenario, select and install storage devices

1. What is the primary advantage of installing an M.2 hard drive directly on the motherboard without using cables?

    A. Faster data transfer rates through the SATA interface

    B. Increased storage capacity through the NVMe interface

    C. Simpler and more secure connection without cable clutter

    D. Compatibility with legacy systems through the IDE interface

2. A user wants to replace the existing hard drive with the fastest possible 1 TB HDD. Which of the following drive types should the technician recommend as the BEST choice?

    A. eSATA

    B. 1TB NVMe SSD

    C. 1TB USB 3.0

    D. 1TB SATA SSD

3. Which of the following RPM options is commonly associated with slower rotational speeds for mechanical hard disk drives (HDDs)?

    A. 5,400 rpm

    B. 7,200 rpm

    C. 10,000 rpm

    D. 15,000 rpm

4. Which type of storage device is commonly used for portable data storage and transfer?

    A. Flash drive

    B. Memory card

    C. Optical drive

    D. Hard disk drive

5. When selecting a motherboard for a specific CPU, what is a critical consideration?

    A. Socket compatibility

    B. Memory type support

    C. Expansion slot availability

    D. Form factor compatibility

6. Which storage device uses laser technology to read and write data on optical disks?

    A. Flash drive

    B. Memory card

    C. Optical drive

    D. Solid-state drive (SSD)

7. How can you identify a SATA cable used in computer hardware?

    A. It has a small, L-shaped connector at one end and a flat connector at the other end

    B. It has a wide, rectangular connector at both ends

    C. It has a round, barrel-shaped connector at one end and a flat connector at the other end

    D. It has a triangular-shaped connector at one end and a small, rectangular connector at the other end

8. Which of the following rpm options is commonly associated with faster rotational speeds for mechanical hard disk drives (HDDs)?

   A. 5,400 rpm

   B. 7,200 rpm

   C. 10,000 rpm

   D. 15,000 rpm

9. You have three hard drives, sized 500 GB, 1 TB, and 2 TB. Which RAID configuration would provide both data redundancy and increased storage capacity?

   A. RAID 0

   B. RAID 1

   C. RAID 5

   D. RAID 10

10. When would you typically use the Peripheral Component Interconnect Express (PCIe) interface in computer hardware?

    A. Connecting high-speed graphics cards

    B. Expanding storage capacity with additional hard drives

    C. Connecting external peripherals such as printers or scanners

    D. Enhancing network connectivity with Wi-Fi or Ethernet adapters

11. You have four hard drives, sized 2 TB, 2 TB, 4 TB, and 4 TB. Which RAID configuration uses a minimum of four drives and would provide both data redundancy and increased storage capacity? (Choose two)

    A. RAID 6

    B. RAID 0

    C. RAID 5

    D. RAID 10

12. You have two hard drives of different sizes, a 1 TB drive and a 500 GB drive. Which RAID configuration would be most suitable for mirroring the data between the drives?

    A. RAID 0

    B. RAID 1

    C. RAID 5

    D. RAID 10

13. Which storage device is commonly used in digital cameras and smartphones for expanding storage capacity?

    A. Flash drive

    B. Memory card

    C. Optical drive

    D. Solid-state drive (SSD)

14. An IT support technician is upgrading their laptop to provide remote administration and run several programs at one time. The read-write speed needs to be the fastest possible. Which of the following options would fulfill their criteria?

    A. 2.5" SAS HDD

    B. M.2 NVMe SSD

    C. 40 GB IDE HDD

    D. mSATA SSD

15. What is a key difference between installing a 2.5" SSD and a 3.5" SSD on a desktop computer?

    A. Form factor and size

    B. Power requirements

    C. Data transfer speed

    D. Compatibility with drive bays

3.4 Given a scenario, install and configure motherboards, central processing units (CPUs), and add-on cards

1. Which of the following statements best describes NVMe compatibility with a motherboard?

    A. NVMe SSDs are compatible with any motherboard that has an M.2 slot

    B. NVMe SSDs are only compatible with older motherboard models

    C. NVMe SSDs require a specific NVMe-compatible motherboard with an M.2 slot

    D. NVMe SSDs can be connected to any SATA port on a motherboard

2. What is the maximum amount of RAM that x86 architecture can support?

    A. 2 GB

    B. 4 GB

    C. 8 GB

    D. 16 GB

3. A user is experiencing an issue where a dual-boot computer does not boot to the desired operating system. Which of the following troubleshooting steps can help resolve this problem?

   A. Check and adjust the boot order in the BIOS settings

   B. Perform a system restore to a previous working state

   C. Install the latest device drivers for the hardware components

   D. Upgrade the computer's RAM for improved performance

4. In a desktop computer, why are heat sinks and fans commonly used?

   A. To minimize the power consumption of the CPU

   B. To reduce the electromagnetic interference (EMI) in the system

   C. To increase the speed of data transfer between components

   D. To dissipate heat and prevent the CPU from overheating

5. In which scenario would you choose to use an ITX form factor for a computer?

   A. Building a compact and portable gaming PC

   B. Setting up a large-scale server farm

   C. Designing a high-performance workstation

   D. Creating a multimedia editing studio

6. What is the primary advantage of liquid cooling over air cooling in a computer system?

   A. Improved thermal efficiency

   B. Quieter operation

   C. Lower cost

   D. Simpler installation

7. After upgrading the motherboard, RAM, and video card, the hard drive is not booting, and the stored data cannot be accessed. The TPM (Trusted Platform Module) is active and hosting the encrypted key. What should the technician do to enable the system to boot again and gain access to the stored data?

   A. Enter the BIOS settings and disable the TPM functionality

   B. Restore the previous motherboard, RAM, and video card configuration

   C. Perform a TPM reset to clear the encryption key and reestablish a secure connection

   D. Contact the TPM manufacturer for guidance on recovering the encrypted data

8. What is a potential cause of a clicking noise when booting up a computer?

    A. Failing hard drive

    B. Overheating CPU

    C. Loose power cable

    D. Malfunctioning graphics card

9. Which of the following power connectors is commonly used to provide power to the CPU on a desktop motherboard?

    A. 8-pin EPS connector

    B. 4-pin Molex connector

    C. 6-pin PCIe connector

    D. 24-pin ATX connector

10. What is a potential consequence of operating a disk infrastructure in a degraded state?

    A. Increased risk of data loss

    B. Decreased power consumption

    C. Improved system performance

    D. Enhanced data security

11. What can happen if the CPU fan fails to function properly?

    A. The CPU may overheat and lead to system instability or shutdown

    B. The CPU's performance may decrease, causing slower operations

    C. The system may emit a loud noise due to increased fan speed

    D. The CPU may become physically damaged

12. When booting up a computer, which component can cause a continuous beeping noise if it is not properly seated?

    A. RAM module

    B. CPU

    C. Power supply unit

    D. Optical drive

13. What is the main difference between AT and ATX motherboards, and which one is considered legacy?

    A. Size and form factor

    B. Power connector design

    C. Expansion slots

    D. RAM type

14. If a heat sink is not effectively dissipating heat from the CPU, what can be done to address the issue?

    A. Check for dust accumulation and clean the heat sink

    B. Replace the thermal paste between the CPU and heat sink

    C. Ensure proper contact between the CPU and heat sink

    D. All of the above

15. A technician inserts an encrypted USB drive protected with BitLocker. When attempting to access the files on the USB drive through File Explorer, the technician encounters an error message stating that the drive is locked. Which of the following tools should the technician use to unlock and gain access to the encrypted drive?

    A. BitLocker Drive Encryption

    B. Disk Clean-up

    C. Windows Defender Firewall

    D. Task Scheduler

16. A student was able to successfully boot from a live Linux CD on a computer in the university library. This resulted in a data breach. Which of the following measures will be the most effective in thwarting this type of attack from occurring in the future?

    A. Implement secure boot and enable BIOS/UEFI password protection

    B. Restrict physical access to the computer and use lockable cabinets

    C. Install and configure a firewall with strict outbound traffic rules

    D. Enforce user access controls and limit administrator privileges

17. When you plug a device into your PC, the power to the PC goes down, and when you detach the device, the power is restored. What is the recommended solution for this situation?

    A. Use a power supply with a higher wattage

    B. Use a power supply with a lower wattage

    C. Use a power supply with better voltage regulation

    D. Use a power supply with a higher amperage

18. Which of the following are potential consequences of a CPU running at high temperatures due to worn thermal paste? (Choose two)

    A. System instability and frequent crashes

    B. Reduced CPU performance and slower system response

    C. Increased power consumption and higher energy costs

    D. Shortened lifespan of the CPU

19. Which of the following methods can improve system performance when multiple applications are being used simultaneously?

    A. Upgrade the RAM to a higher capacity

    B. Close unnecessary background processes and applications

    C. Install a faster solid-state drive (SSD)

    D. Increase the CPU clock speed

20. Which of the following options correctly describes a Molex connector?

    A. The Molex connector is used to provide power to SATA drives

    B. The Molex connector is primarily used for connecting fans and cooling devices

    C. The Molex connector is a standard power connector for motherboards

    D. The Molex connector is used to connect USB devices to the computer

21. What type of disk infrastructure is typically used in a degraded state?

    A. RAID (Redundant Array of Independent Disks)

    B. SATA (Serial ATA) disks

    C. SSD (Solid-State Drive) disks

    D. External USB disks

22. What is a potential cause when some keys on the keyboard do not work and there is no sign of physical damage?

    A. Software compatibility issues

    B. Incorrect keyboard layout settings

    C. Outdated keyboard drivers

    D. BIOS settings misconfiguration

23. What is the primary purpose of setting a boot password in a computer's BIOS settings?

    A. To prevent unauthorized access to the computer's BIOS settings

    B. To encrypt the data on the computer's hard drive

    C. To enhance the overall system performance

    D. To optimize the boot process for faster startup

24. What is the primary purpose of a Hardware Security Module (HSM)?

    A. Securely store and manage cryptographic keys

    B. Improve network performance

    C. Provide virtual machine encryption

    D. Enhance multi-threading capabilities

25. What is the purpose of multithreading in computer systems?

    A. Increase parallel processing and improve performance

    B. Provide secure storage for sensitive data

    C. Virtualize hardware resources for multiple applications

    D. Enhance network connectivity and speed

26. What should you do if virtual machines are not working on your computer, and you need to troubleshoot the issue?

    A. Update the BIOS firmware to the latest version

    B. Enable the "Virtualization Technology," "Intel VT-x," or "AMD-V" options in the BIOS settings

    C. Ensure that your computer meets the hardware requirements for running virtual machines

    D. Verify that the necessary drivers for virtualization are installed and up to date

27. What is the primary advantage of advanced risk computing?

    A. Improved performance and efficiency

    B. Enhanced security and data protection

    C. Increased scalability and flexibility

    D. Reduced power consumption and environmental impact

28. Which of the following best describes the purpose of Intel architecture in advanced computing?

    A. Enabling high-performance computing applications

    B. Providing advanced encryption and data security

    C. Facilitating cloud computing and virtualization

    D. Enhancing artificial intelligence and machine learning capabilities

29. What is a key benefit of multicore processors in advanced computing?

    A. Increased parallel processing capabilities

    B. Enhanced single-threaded performance

    C. Improved power efficiency and heat management

    D. Expanded memory capacity and bandwidth

30. For which type of devices are Intel Core M processors specifically designed?

    A. High-performance desktop computers

    B. Ultra-thin notebooks, tablets

    C. Gaming consoles and graphics-intensive systems

    D. Enterprise servers and data centers

3.5 Given a scenario, install or replace the appropriate power supply

1. When should you consider using a modular power supply in a desktop computer?

    A. When you want to improve cable management and reduce clutter

    B. When you need a power supply with a higher wattage capacity

    C. When you want to enhance system cooling and airflow

    D. When you require a power supply with multiple voltage outputs

2. In the event of a power failure, what is the purpose of replacing a redundant power supply in a computer system?

    A. Ensures an uninterrupted power supply

    B. Increases storage capacity

    C. Enhances CPU performance

    D. Improves network connectivity

3. When considering voltage levels for input and output connections, which of the following options correctly represents the typical voltage ranges for 3.3V, 5V, and 12V, along with their associated wire color?

    A. 3.3V: Orange or yellow; 5V: Red; 12V: Yellow or blue

    B. 3.3V: Red; 5V: Yellow; 12V: Orange or blue

    C. 3.3V: Blue; 5V: Red; 12V: Yellow or orange

    D. 3.3V: Yellow or orange; 5V: Red; 12V: Blue

4. Which type of standard motherboard typically uses a 20-pin or 24-pin power connector?

    A. ATX (Advanced Technology eXtended)

    B. Mini-ITX (Information Technology eXtended)

    C. Micro-ATX (Advanced Technology eXtended)

    D. ITX (Information Technology eXtended)

5. What is the primary advantage of a modular power supply?

    A. Customizable cable management

    B. Higher efficiency

    C. Enhanced cooling performance

    D. Increased power output

6. When selecting the appropriate voltage input for electrical devices, which of the following options represents the correct voltage ranges for 110-120 VAC and 220-240 VAC?

    A. 110-120 VAC: Standard voltage in North America; 220-240 VAC: Standard voltage in Europe

    B. 110-120 VAC: Standard voltage in Europe; 220-240 VAC: Standard voltage in North America

    C. 10-120 VAC: Standard voltage for high-power devices; 220-240 VAC: Standard voltage for low-power devices

    D. 110-120 VAC: Standard voltage for low-power devices; 220-240 VAC: Standard voltage for high-power devices

7. In an office environment where power failures can disrupt operations, what is the recommended solution to ensure a continuous power supply?

    A. Implement a redundant power supply system

    B. Increase the number of power outlets

    C. Upgrade the office furniture

    D. Install backup generators

8. What wattage is the recommended power supply for a typical desktop computer?

    A. 300 W

    B. 500 W

    C. 750 W

    D. 1,000 W

3.6 Given a scenario, deploy and configure multifunction devices/printers and settings

1. A company is experiencing an issue with its dot matrix printer that uses carbon paper. They report that the print on the first page is too light, while the subsequent pages are still legible. What is the most likely cause of this problem?

    A. The print head pins are worn out, resulting in inconsistent printing

    B. The carbon paper is not aligned properly in the printer, causing the first page to print lighter

    C. The printer driver needs to be updated to ensure optimal printing quality

    D. The printer's power supply is not providing sufficient voltage to the print head

2. What happens during the charging stage of a laser printer?

    A. Toner particles are attracted to the charged areas on the drum

    B. The laser beam scans the photosensitive drum, creating an electrostatic image

    C. Any residual toner or debris is removed from the drum and other components

    D. The primary corona wire charges the photosensitive drum uniformly

3. Which type of printer typically uses a laser beam or LED light source for image formation?

    A. Laser printer

    B. Dot matrix printer

    C. Thermal printer

    D. Impact printer

4. When using the scan-to-email feature on a multifunction device (MFD), what configuration is required to send the scanned document as an email attachment?

    A. Configuring the MFD with the IP address of an SMTP server

    B. Enabling Wi-Fi connectivity on the MFD

    C. Installing email client software on the MFD

    D. Connecting the MFD to a network printer

5. What is the purpose of a print server?

    A. To manage the printing process and control print jobs

    B. To provide network connectivity for printers

    C. To share printers and enable print jobs from multiple computers

    D. To store and manage printer drivers

6. You notice that unauthorized individuals are using the printer without permission. This has resulted in the printer paper budget doubling in size. What should be implemented to address this security concern and reduce the paper budget?

    A. User authentication and access control

    B. Regular printer maintenance

    C. Printer driver update

    D. Network connection troubleshooting

7. Which type of printer uses a series of pins striking an inked ribbon to create images?

    A. Laser printer

    B. Dot matrix printer

    C. Thermal printer

    D. Impact printer

8. Which of the following is the correct sequence of a laser printer?

    A. Charging, exposing, developing, transferring, fusing, and cleaning

    B. Cleaning, exposing, developing, transferring, fusing, and charging

    C. Charging, exposing, developing, fusing, transferring, and cleaning

    D. Cleaning, exposing, developing, transferring, and fusing

9. Which type of printer generates images by applying heat to special heat-sensitive paper that needs to be kept out of direct sunlight?

    A. Laser printer

    B. Dot matrix printer

    C. Thermal printer

    D. Impact printer

10. What could be the issue if printed documents have poor print quality? (Choose two)

    A. The printer is low on ink or toner

    B. The paper quality is low

    C. The printer driver needs to be updated

    D. The printer settings are incorrect

11. What happens during the fusing stage of a laser printer?

    A. The toner on the paper is fused and melted into the fibers

    B. Toner particles are attracted to the charged areas on the drum

    C. Any residual toner or debris is removed from the drum and other components

    D. The laser beam scans the photosensitive drum, creating an electrostatic image

12. You have a printer with two paper trays – the top tray contains paper, and the bottom tray contains labels. You notice that when printing, the documents are printed on labels instead of paper. What could be the issue? (Choose two)

    A. The top paper tray has run out of paper

    B. The paper tray selection is wrong

    C. The printer driver needs to be updated

    D. The ink or toner is low

13. How can a printer in a SOHO obtain the same IP from a wireless router running DHCP?

    A. Enable DHCP reservation

    B. Configure a static IP address for the printer

    C. Restart the router regularly

    D. Use a USB cable for network connectivity

14. When using the scan-to-folder feature on a multifunction device (MFD), what configuration is required to save the scanned document as a file on a shared network folder?

    A. Configuring the MFD with the path to a suitably configured file server and shared folder

    B. Enabling Bluetooth connectivity on the MFD

    C. Installing file compression software on the MFD

    D. Connecting the MFD to a USB storage device

15. When using the scan-to-cloud feature on a multifunction device (MFD), what does it mean to scan to the cloud?

    A. Uploading the scan as a file to a document storage and sharing account in the cloud

    B. Sending the scan as an email attachment to a cloud service provider

    C. Printing the scan directly from the MFD to a cloud-based printer

    D. Saving the scan on a local network server accessible from the cloud

16. You are experiencing issues where many print jobs are not getting picked up from the printer's paper trays. What can be implemented to prevent this issue?

    A. Enable printing only when authorized users insert a PIN

    B. Printer driver update

    C. Clearing the print queue and restarting the printer

    D. Replacing the printer's ink or toner cartridges

3.7 Given a scenario, install and replace the printer consumables

1. Which component is responsible for the charging stage in a laser printer?

    A. Toner cartridge

    B. Drum unit

    C. Corona wire

    D. Fuser assembly

2. Which type of USB connector is commonly used for connecting printers to a computer?

    A. Type A

    B. Type B

    C. Type C

    D. Micro-USB

3. What could be the issue if a printed document is coming out landscape instead of portrait? How can we resolve this issue?

   A. The printer driver is outdated

   B. The wrong printer settings are selected

   C. The printer's ink or toner is low

   D. The paper size is incorrect

4. When connecting a USB printer to a computer running Windows 10, what is the most important step to ensure proper functionality?

   A. Selecting the appropriate printer model

   B. Installing the latest printer driver compatible with Windows 10

   C. Ensuring the USB cable is securely connected to both the printer and the computer

   D. Configuring the printer settings to match the desired paper size

5. How does wireless printing work in a network with multiple printers?

   A. Each printer has its own dedicated Wi-Fi network for wireless printing

   B. The printers are connected to a central print server that handles wireless print jobs

   C. Each printer is assigned a unique IP address and communicates directly with devices on the network

   D. Devices must physically connect to each printer using a USB cable for wireless printing

6. Which type of 3D printing technology is commonly used with liquid resin materials?

   A. Fused Deposition Modeling (FDM)

   B. Stereolithography (SLA)

   C. Selective Laser Sintering (SLS)

   D. Digital Light Processing (DLP)

7. Which of the following steps is required to set up print sharing and enable multiple computers to use a shared printer? (Select all that apply)

   A. Connect the printer to a computer acting as the print server

   B. Install the necessary printer drivers on each computer

   C. Enable printer sharing in the printer's properties on the print server computer

   D. Access the network settings on client computers and select the shared printer

   E. Test the print-sharing functionality by sending a print job from a client computer

8. When would you typically use Printer Control Language (PCL) in printing?

    A. Printing documents with complex graphics and images

    B. Printing text-based documents without complex formatting

    C. Printing high-resolution photographs and images

    D. Printing documents with advanced font rendering and color management

9. When unboxing a new print device, which of the following actions should you perform? (Choose three)

    A. Remove all protective tapes and packaging materials

    B. A print device should normally be left to acclimate after removing the packaging materials

    C. Install the necessary software and drivers

    D. Load paper and adjust paper settings

    E. Use a two-person lift technique for the printer

    F. Perform a test print to ensure functionality

10. To replace the filament in a 3D printer, which of the following actions should the technician take? (Choose two)

    A. Heat the extruder to a specific temperature to soften the filament and remove it manually

    B. Navigate to the printer's settings menu and select "Filament Replacement"

    C. Pull as much of the old filament out as possible, then push the new filament through

    D. Use a specialized tool to unscrew the filament spool and replace it

11. Which type of 3D printing technology uses filament materials such as ABS or PLA?

    A. Fused Deposition Modeling (FDM)

    B. Stereolithography (SLA)

    C. Selective Laser Sintering (SLS)

    D. Digital Light Processing (DLP)

12. How does Wi-Fi direct printing work?

    A. The printer connects directly to a Wi-Fi network for wireless printing

    B. The printer creates its own Wi-Fi network for devices to connect and print wirelessly

    C. The printer requires a physical connection to a device for wireless printing

    D. The printer uses Bluetooth technology for wireless printing

13. What components are typically included in a printer maintenance kit?

    A. New fuser assembly, transfer/secondary charge roller, and paper transport rollers

    B. New toner cartridges and cleaning sheets

    C. Replacement ink cartridges and printheads

    D. Additional paper trays and feeder units

14. When would you typically use PostScript in printing?

    A. Printing documents with complex graphics and images

    B. Printing text-based documents without complex formatting

    C. Printing high-resolution photographs and images

    D. Printing documents with advanced font rendering and color management

4

Virtualization and Cloud Computing

Introduction

A new trend in the IT industry has seen an increasing number of companies moving their data online, taking advantage of the more cost-effective cloud and its features. Cloud computing refers to the provisioning of resources without the need for capital expenditure, in which the **Cloud Service Provider (CSP)** provides all of the hardware and customer lease access. The CSP is also responsible for disaster recovery, so that the customer only pays for the resources that they use.

Virtualization has also become increasingly popular within companies due to the ability to recover a desktop or server in minutes. Prior to virtualization, if a server crashed, it could take the system administrator half a day to recover it. Virtualization is used to provide desktops for cloud computers.

In the CompTIA A+ Core 1 (220-1101) certification examination, Domain 4.0 Virtualization and Cloud Computing makes up 11% of the assessment and is broken down into the following exam objectives:

- 4.1 Summarize cloud computing concepts
- 4.2 Summarize aspects of client-side virtualization

The rest of this chapter is committed to practice. For each of the previously defined concepts, you will be given a series of questions designed to test your knowledge of each core 1 objective as defined by the official certification exam guidance for this domain. Once you have completed these questions and ensured you understand the concepts behind them, you should be fully prepared to do the same on your CompTIA A+ Core 1 (220-1101) exam.

Practice Exam Questions

4.1 Summarize cloud computing concepts

1. What type of cloud service would you use if you wanted to move 100 desktops to the cloud?

   A. SaaS

   B. IaaS

   C. SECaaS

   D. MaaS

2. In which type of cloud model does a company have most of its workforce on-premises and its mobile salesforce in the cloud?

   A. Hybrid

   B. Private

   C. Community

   D. Public

3. An organization is expanding, and it needs to increase its storage space and compute resources to meet the demand of its customers. Most of the workforce operates as remote workers. Which of the following best describes the cloud service required?

   A. PaaS

   B. SaaS

   C. IaaS

   D. DRaas

4. A company wants to migrate its email and business applications to the cloud. Which of the following cloud services will be used to meet the objective?

   A. PaaS

   B. SaaS

   C. IaaS

   D. MaaS

5. The Chief Executive Officer wants to ensure that when the company moves to the cloud, it retains total control over the storage and management of proprietary data. Which cloud model is the best for this?

   A. Hybrid cloud

   B. Community cloud

   C. Public cloud

   D. Private cloud

6. A salesperson from a Cloud Service Provider (CSP) is trying to sell a company metered utilization as part of a cloud package. Which of the following describes what they are selling?

   A. Unlimited resources for free

   B. A reserve pool of resources

   C. Pay only for the resources consumed

   D. Restriction on the allocation of critical resources

7. Which of the following cloud models would allow three universities to share resources in a cloud environment?

   A. Private cloud

   B. Public cloud

   C. Community cloud

   D. Hybrid cloud

8. A company is going to employ two consultants to help with data migration. The consultants will be able to connect to the desktops that the company allocates through a thin client to prevent anyone from downloading the company data. The configuration of each desktop must remain consistent. Which of the following will the IT team roll out to meet their needs and ensure the company has total control over the data?

   A. Surface laptops

   B. VDI

   C. Terminal servers

   D. IaaS

9. A company would like to enable its developers to create bespoke applications. These applications will require two separate servers, one for PHP and the other for MySQL. What cloud service should they purchase?

    A. SaaS

    B. IaaS

    C. PaaS

    D. Private cloud

10. What type of cloud model is known as multi-tenant?

    A. Private

    B. Community

    C. Hybrid

    D. Public

11. A law firm is going to migrate its currently on-premises infrastructure to the cloud. The firm stores a large number of wills and probates, property, and trust deeds. This data must be retained for a minimum of six years. What type of cloud model best fits this law firm's needs?

    A. Public cloud

    B. Private cloud

    C. Hybrid cloud

    D. Community cloud

12. Which of the following describes why a cloud provider would store hardware in its data center that is not dedicated to any single customer?

    A. Dynamic resource allocation

    B. Backup pool

    C. Shared resources

    D. System sprawl

13. Which of the following means that the server experiences very little downtime (also known as the "five nines")?

   A. VDI

   B. High Availability (HA)

   C. Clustering

   D. Shared resources

14. A famous toy company sees an increase in sales over the winter holidays and, consequently, needs to purchase more VDI and CPU resources to match customer demand leading up to Christmas. However, they need to be able to revert to normal resource consumption in January. What aspect of cloud computing would the toy company find useful?

   A. Shared resources

   B. Clustering

   C. Rapid elasticity

   D. Metered utilization

15. What type of cloud allows access to data even if the internet fails?

   A. Private

   B. Community

   C. SaaS

   D. Public

16. What type of cloud service is VDI?

   A. SaaS

   B. DaaS

   C. PaaS

   D. IaaS

17. What type of cloud model is known as single-tenant?

   A. Hybrid

   B. Private

   C. Community

   D. Public

18. Which of the following are only SaaS products? (Choose two)

    A. Office 365

    B. Developer tools

    C. Home Depot

    D. Spotify

19. Due to COVID, a financial company is moving all its workers to a work-from-home model. The company must ensure that stringent financial regulations are enforced at all times and that they can control users' desktops and prevent the exfiltration of data. Which of the following solutions will the company implement?

    A. VDI

    B. SaaS

    C. VPN

    D. RDP

20. Which of the following is an automated advantage of cloud storage?

    A. Resource exhaustion

    B. Dynamic resource allocation

    C. File sharing

    D. File synchronization

21. What is one of the disadvantages of using VDI on-premises?

    A. Recovering a virtual desktop using a snapshot is very slow

    B. Network failure means that no local processing of data can take place

    C. The connection can be achieved by using Citrix

    D. Disaster recovery is provided by the cloud provider

22. An IT company is going to move 10 servers and 50 desktops to the cloud. Which of the following cloud services will they migrate to?

    A. PaaS

    B. SaaS

    C. MaaS

    D. IaaS

23. New Zealand has just won the rugby World Cup final, and the official All Blacks online store cannot cope with the number of New Zealanders wanting to purchase their World Cup memorabilia. The store manager contacts their cloud provider for additional resources, which the cloud provider adds within 30 minutes. Which of the following concepts BEST describes what the cloud provider has just done?

   A. Rapid deployment

   B. Rapid elasticity

   C. Load balancing

   D. Metered service

4.2 Summarize aspects of client-side virtualization

1. What type of hypervisor runs on a bare-metal virtual platform?

   A. Type 1

   B. Type 2

   C. Type 3

   D. Type 4

2. A company is using VMware's ESX Server to provide its virtual network. It will be running five database servers, each of which will require an increase in CPU and RAM. How can this be achieved?

   A. Resource pooling

   B. System sprawl

   C. Network segmentation

   D. Metered utilization

3. An attacker gained access to a vulnerable guest computer and managed to attack the hypervisor, which resulted in a total failure of the virtual network. What type of attack was carried out?

   A. Pivoting

   B. VM sprawl

   C. Snapshot

   D. VM escape

4. What type of hypervisors will Oracle VirtualBox for Windows 10 run on?

    A. Type 3

    B. Type 2

    C. Type 5

    D. Type 1

5. What are the THREE main reasons that an IT team would create a sandbox?

    A. To help prevent fires from spreading

    B. To test new versions of software

    C. To test new hardware

    D. To examine applications that potentially contain malware

    E. To ensure that new software patches do not have an adverse effect on business applications

6. A manufacturer of pressure-relieving mattresses has a legacy application that tests cell movement. It needs to run on a Windows 98 operating system, which is a legacy system that is no longer supported. The company is updating all of the servers to Server 2022, with Windows 11 desktops, and plans to outsource the rewriting of the legacy application so that it is Windows 11 compliant. What should the manufacturer do in the meantime? (Choose two)

    A. Build a Linux workstation and use it to run the legacy application

    B. Create a sandbox for the legacy application

    C. Build a virtual machine with the Windows 98 operating system

    D. Install Hyper-V on one of the Windows 11 desktops in the manufacturing department

    E. Install the application on a SQL server

7. What is the purpose of using Second Level Address Translation (SLAT)?

    A. It improves the performance of virtual memory when multiple guest machines are installed

    B. It improves the performance of virtual networking when multiple guest machines are installed

    C. It prevents the use of virtual memory when multiple guest machines are installed

    D. It throttles the processor on multiple guest machines

8. Which of the following describes cross-platform virtualization?

   A. Installing virtual machines on Hyper-V, ESX, and Xen

   B. Installing and networking multiple sandboxes

   C. Testing multiple software applications, one after another, in a single sandbox

   D. Testing software applications under multiple operating systems and workloads

9. A company has a virtual network running 10 host machines, each with 50 guest machines. Yesterday, an attacker successfully connected to the host's physical network card and exchanged packets directly with a guest operating system, bypassing the host operating system. Which of the following BEST describes how the attacker gained access?

   A. The attacker used a NAT

   B. The attacker joined the local area network of the host

   C. The attacker used a virtual private network

   D. The attacker used a bridged network

10. A university professor teaches a computer class 10 times a week. The professor wants to ensure that they have a rapid solution to set the desktops up for their next group at the end of each session. To do this, they plan to build a master image of the operating system that can be rolled out so that all desktops will reset once the students have logged off. Which of the following technologies should the professor implement? (Choose two)

    A. They should create a ghost image so that they can reimage each machine

    B. They need to build a virtual machine environment and take a snapshot

    C. They need to take a system image and roll it out between classes

    D. They need to create a data backup

    E. They need to implement a VDI environment that utilizes VDE

11. Which of the following BEST describes virtual machine sprawl?

    A. A virtual machine overutilizing resources

    B. An isolation virtual machine for application testing

    C. An unmanaged virtual machine on the network

    D. The host machine is running out of resources due to overconsumption

12. A system administrator plans to implement VDI and wants to ensure that the storage for the virtual machine is both fault tolerant and has fast disk access. Which of the following should the administrator implement to fulfill these requirements?

    A. RAID 0 using SSD

    B. LAN

    C. Fiber Channel SAN

    D. RAID 5 using HDDs

13. If you wanted to separate a guest machine from the host or another virtual machine, which of the following would you implement?

    A. DMZ

    B. Isolation

    C. Docker

    D. Snapshot

14. A company's virtual network has been flooded with rogue virtual machines, which were not been patched when the other virtual machines were updated. This is a security risk as these unmanaged devices could be used to gain access to the company's network. The company has now employed a security consultant to remedy the situation. Which of the following is the consultant most likely to recommend? (Choose two)

    A. Deploy virtual machines using an image template

    B. Install anti-virus software on unmanaged virtual machines

    C. Deploy SolarWinds Virtualization Manager

    D. Remove the unmanaged virtual machines

15. A network administrator plans to deploy another virtual host server with 15 TB of memory and quad processors onto their virtual network. However, after building the host server, they find that the hypervisor fails to run. Which of the following is the BEST choice to resolve this issue?

    A. VT-x

    B. Multi-cores

    C. VT-d

    D. Intel GVT

16. Why would a network administrator ensure they use an Uninterruptible Power Supply (UPS) when deploying a new virtual host server? (Choose two)

    A. It provides power for the virtual host in the event of total power loss

    B. It provides power for the virtual host for 5 minutes so that the host can be shut down gracefully

    C. It provides temporary power for the virtual host should there be a power loss for a few seconds

    D. It provides power for booting the virtual host

17. What is the benefit of using container virtualization?

    A. It allows you to create a virtual machine backup

    B. It allows you to test malware

    C. It allows you to separate your applications from the infrastructure and deploy and test code rapidly

    D. It prevents virtual machine escape

18. What is application virtualization?

    A. Putting an application into a sandbox for testing

    B. Installing an application locally on a virtual machine

    C. Putting the application inside a container

    D. Running an application from a remote server that has additional resources

5

Hardware and Network Troubleshooting

Introduction

Understanding the importance of hardware and network troubleshooting is vital for any IT professional. Efficient troubleshooting minimizes downtime, optimizes system performance, and extends the lifespan of hardware. It enhances the user experience, safeguards data and security, and builds a reputation for reliability and expertise. Moreover, mastering troubleshooting opens doors to career advancement and equips you to handle emergencies with confidence. Throughout this chapter, you'll gain practical knowledge to tackle various hardware and network challenges, empowering you as a skilled problem solver in the dynamic world of IT.

In the CompTIA A+ Core 1 (220-1101) certification examination, Domain 5.0 Hardware and Network Troubleshooting makes up 27% of the assessment and is further broken down into the following exam objectives:

- 5.1 Given a scenario, apply the best practice methodology to resolve problems

- 5.2 Given a scenario, troubleshoot problems related to motherboards, RAM, CPU, and power

- 5.3 Given a scenario, troubleshoot and diagnose problems with storage drives and RAID arrays

- 5.4 Given a scenario, troubleshoot video, projector, and display issues

- 5.5 Given a scenario, troubleshoot common issues with mobile devices

- 5.6 Given a scenario, troubleshoot and resolve printer issues

- 5.7 Given a scenario, troubleshoot problems with wired and wireless networks

The rest of this chapter is committed to practice. For each of the concepts defined above, you will be given a series of questions designed to test your knowledge of each core 1 objective as defined by the official certification exam guidance for this domain. Once you have completed these questions and ensured you understand the concepts behind them, you should be fully prepared to do the same on your CompTIA A+ Core 1 (220-1101) exam.

Practice Exam Questions

5.1 Given a scenario, apply the best-practice methodology to resolve the problem

1. A systems administrator is given a ticket by the help desk to deal with the chief executive officer's printer. Their secretary said that it will not print, a light is flashing, and they think the printer paper is the issue. What should the systems administrator do first?

    A. Verify the printer's full system functionality

    B. Test a theory to determine the cause of the printer issue

    C. Identify the problem with the printer

    D. Establish a plan of action to resolve the email server issue

2. A junior administrator was given a verbal warning by the IT manager following an incident where they patched the exchange server during working hours. This resulted in rebooting the server and 600 users not having access to their email for 15 minutes. Which of the following BEST describes the junior administrator's actions?

    A. Patch management

    B. Poor communication with users

    C. Standard operating procedure violation

    D. Establishing a plan of action

3. A user has a problem with their laptop and a second-line support technician has arrived. The support technician knows that they must try and identify the problem. Which of the following should the support technician do first? (Choose two)

    A. Back up all of the data

    B. Ask the user whether they made any recent changes

    C. Ask the user what they were doing before the incident occurred

    D. Search the vendor's website for guidance

4. A systems administrator took 4 hours to identify and then implement a solution. The systems administrator then implemented the repair and tested full functionality. What should the administrator do next?

   A. Establish a theory of probable cause

   B. Implement preventative measures

   C. Document the findings, actions, and outcomes in the call center database

   D. Test the theory to determine the cause

5. A system administrator has determined that a user's laptop has the wrong screen resolution. They believe that a recent Windows update has caused the problem. What stage in the troubleshooting process have they just carried out?

   A. Establishing a theory of probable cause

   B. Identifying the problem

   C. Establishing a plan of action

   D. Testing the theory to determine the cause

5.2 Given a scenario, troubleshoot problems related to motherboards, RAM, CPU, and power

1. What safety precautions should I take when replacing Random Access Memory (RAM) on Windows Server 2022? (Choose two)

   A. Hot-swap the RAM

   B. Turn off the power

   C. Put the machine in standby mode

   D. Wear an electromagnetic static wrist strap

2. A user raises a ticket with the help desk as their desktop computer will not start. On arrival, the computer technician reboots the computer, and it beeps continuously. Which of the following is the problem with the desktop computer?

   A. A motherboard problem

   B. A RAM problem

   C. A power supply problem

   D. A video adapter problem

3. A computer technician needs to upgrade the Central Processing Unit (CPU) in an AutoCAD computer. What is the first thing they should do?

   A. Turn off the power

   B. Search the manufacturer's website for the socket type

   C. Wear an electromagnetic static wrist strap

   D. Back up the data

4. A computer technician has just installed additional RAM in a desktop computer and it has not been recognized. What should the computer technician do next? (Choose two)

   A. Check the computer's BIOS

   B. Wear an electromagnetic static wrist strap

   C. Reboot the computer

   D. Reseat the memory modules

5. A computer technician has received a desktop computer from the customer services department. The customer services technician stated that the desktop computer recently had maintenance carried out by the second-line technician. They plug the computer into the main power but when they switch the desktop computer on, there is a black screen. They can hear the internal fans spinning, so they know there is power to the desktop computer. Which of the following could have caused this error? (Choose two)

   A. An incorrectly orientated storage adapter cable

   B. A motherboard error

   C. The computer monitor is not switched on

   D. A faulty Power Supply Unit (PSU)

6. A user has complained to the help desk that the time on her computer is inaccurate. She has changed the time twice in the last week, but the computer clock keeps falling behind. The system administrator arrives and confirms that the clock time is inaccurate. What should the system administrator do to rectify the problem?

   A. Change the power cable to the computer

   B. Change the PSU

   C. Change the complementary metal-oxide semiconductor (CMOS) battery

   D. Search on the manufacturer's website to see whether there is an update to the BIOS

7. A computer technician is carrying out annual maintenance on a desktop computer. When inspecting the motherboard, they notice that one of the capacitors is swollen. They take the computer back to their repair room to replace the capacitor. What is the purpose of capacitors located on the motherboard?

    A. The capacitor circulates the airflow

    B. The capacitor prevents power spikes

    C. The capacitor stores data

    D. The capacitor is used to power the real-time clock

8. A user was issued with a new laptop computer running Windows 10. They raised a ticket with the help desk as their fingerprint reader is now not working following a recent Windows update. Which of the following is the next step?

    A. Update the BIOS

    B. Clear the Trusted Platform Module (TPM)

    C. Restore a system image

    D. Reboot the laptop

9. A computer technician is diagnosing a problem with a desktop computer. When they reboot the computer, they hear 1 long beep, followed by 2 short beeps. What does the computer technician diagnose the problem as?

    A. A motherboard problem

    B. A normal post

    C. A power supply problem

    D. A video adapter problem

10. A computer technician has just been called out to the customer services department as one of the desktop computers has no power. The computer technician pushes the power button and there is no power and they cannot hear any noise from the internal fans. Which of the following should the computer technician carry out when diagnosing the problem? (Choose three)

    A. Check the plug socket is turned on

    B. Change the memory modules

    C. Replace the power cable

    D. Plug a lamp into the power socket

11. What has caused the following problem? (Choose two)

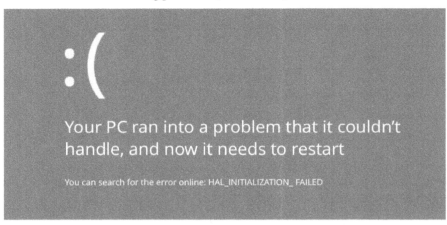

Your PC ran into a problem that it couldn't handle, and now it needs to restart

You can search for the error online: HAL_INITIALIZATION_ FAILED

   A. A system memory fault

   B. A motherboard problem

   C. An operating system corruption

   D. A RAM problem

12. A user has reported to the help desk that they can smell burning coming from their computer. The help desk technician tells the user to immediately turn off the computer and unplug the power from the wall socket. Which of the following could have caused the burning smell? (Select all that apply)

   A. The CPU fan is not working

   B. The heatsink is not fitted properly

   C. The PSU is overheating

   D. The fan vents are clogged with dust

13. Which of the following could cause a computer to perform "sluggishly"?

   A. The keyboard is not plugged in

   B. A recent configuration has been made incorrectly

   C. The mouse is not connected

   D. The computer has no CPU

14. Which of the following would produce a grinding noise? (Choose two)

    A. A problem with the RAM

    B. A problem with a toner cartridge on an inkjet printer

    C. A problem with the hard drive

    D. A problem with the motherboard

15. A user reports to the help desk that they are having problems with their keyboard. The keyboard appears to be undamaged but when the computer technician tried the keyboard, some letters were not working. What should the computer technician do first?

    A. Vacuum the keyboard

    B. Wipe the keyboard with a wet cloth

    C. Clean the keyboard with compressed air

    D. Disable sticky keys

5.3 Given a scenario, troubleshoot and diagnose problems with storage drives and RAID arrays

1. A customer has called an IT support company to provide a storage solution to a customer. The customer has purchased three 20-TB hard drives and the solution must provide fast read access and redundancy. Which of the following solutions would be the best to implement?

    A. RAID 0

    B. RAID 1

    C. RAID 5

    D. RAID 6

2. A system administrator receives an alert from their mail server that one of the disks has failed. They log in to the server and can only see four out of their five disk sets. They have a hardware RAID 5 solution and therefore they can hot-swap out the failed disk. What risk if, any, will the system administrator encounter when replacing the failed disk?

    A. RAID 5 is redundant and there is no risk at all

    B. Pull the disks out one at a time and look for the SCSI ID of the failed disk

    C. Look on the RAID array and look for the disk with the red light

    D. If you remove a healthy disk, you will lose all your data

3. A user boots up their computer and receives the following SMART error:

> SMART Hard Disk Error
> The SMART hard disk check has detected an imminent failure
> Please backup the content immediately and run Hard Disk Test

What should the user do next?

A. Launch "Advanced > SMART settings > SMART self-test"

B. Go to Disk Management and format the disk to get rid of errors

C. Swap out the disk for a new disk

D. Disable SMART monitoring

4. A computer technician is trying to find out why a computer cannot boot. They take out the hard disk and connect it to a computer with recovery software. They are able to see the data. What should the computer technician do next?

A. Put the disk back into the computer and boot from it

B. Format the disk using Disk Management

C. Back up the data

D. Put the disk back into the computer and then install the recovery software

5. A manager is working from their laptop computer and installs an encrypted USB drive containing a number of Excel spreadsheets that are confidential. They raise a ticket with the help disk. A support technician arrives to resolve the problem. What will the technician do to resolve the issue?

A. They will use Disk Management

B. They will convert the USB into New Technology File System (NTFS)

C. They will turn on BitLocker on the C drive

D. They will turn on BitLocker on the USB drive

6. A computer technician is receiving disk errors from SMART monitoring. The computer boots normally and when they look at disk management, it states that all disks are in a healthy state. What is the cause of this error?

A. Disk management is not functioning properly

B. The filesystem is NTFS

C. SMART monitoring is malfunctioning

D. A disk is missing from the RAID 5 system

7. A user's computer fails to boot up and they notice the hard drive LED is a solid orange. Which of the following could be causing this issue?

    A. The computer has a memory problem

    B. There is a hardware problem with the hard disk drive

    C. The computer has a processor problem

    D. SMART monitoring has been disabled, causing the computer to freeze

8. A computer technician runs a performance test against a computer's hard drive. The test reveals that the disk is suffering from extended read/write times. What should the technician do next?

    A. Launch "Advanced > SMART settings > SMART self-test"

    B. Run the system diagnostic program that was supplied with the computer

    C. Swap out the disk with a new disk

    D. Disable SMART monitoring

9. A computer that is configured with RAID 5 receives an alert that one of the disks is in a degraded state. Which of the following is causing this error and how does it affect the data on the disk? (Choose two)

    A. One of the disks in the RAID 5 set needs to be formatted to NTFS

    B. One of the disks in the RAID 5 set has failed

    C. The data is no longer available

    D. The data is still available

10. A computer technician boots up a computer and gets the error message "missing operating system." Which of the following is causing this error?

    A. There is a disk missing from a RAID set

    B. The computer is having a Windows update

    C. The disk with the operating system has failed

    D. The CMOS battery is failing

11. How can you tell if a storage device's performance is degrading?

    A. There will be a solid orange light

    B. Check the IOPS

    C. Check Disk Management

    D. There will be a flashing green light

5.4 Given a scenario, troubleshoot video, projector, and display issues

1. A technician has been called to a classroom as the projector is very dim. Which of the following is causing the problem?

    A. The inverter is broken

    B. They need to adjust the display settings

    C. The digitizer is failing

    D. A burned-out bulb

2. A technician is setting up a projector in a conference room and gets an error saying "no signal." What could be the cause of this issue?

    A. The cable to the projector is faulty and needs to be replaced

    B. The projectors' bulb needs to be replaced

    C. The computer's monitor is broken

    D. The computer needs to have its display set to "extend this display"

3. A professor at a university connects their laptop to the projector in a theatre. The image being projected is fuzzy. Which of the following is causing this issue?

    A. The cable is defective

    B. The laptop display setting needs to be adjusted

    C. The projector lens needs to be adjusted

    D. The projector bulb needs to be replaced

4. A presenter is trying to play a video that is on a DVD in their laptop. They can hear the sound but get an error on the projector stating "COPY PROTECTION: THE DVI/HDMI OUTPUT IS BLOCKED." Which of the following is causing this issue?

    A. The HDMI cable is faulty

    B. The protector is not HDCP-compatible

    C. The display settings need to be adjusted

    D. There is a problem with the DVD player

5. A computer technician has connected a laptop to a projector in a lecture hall but an image is not being projected on the screen. They go back to their workshop and bring cables that they know are working. After swapping the cables, they get a "no source found" error. What should the computer technician do next? (Choose two)

    A. Replace the projector's bulb

    B. Check the connection on the HDMI cable

    C. Run displayswitch.exe and select either duplicate or extend

    D. Go to display settings on the laptop, choose multiple displays, and duplicate these displays

6. A computer technician has been called out to a conference room where a presentation is due to take place. The presenter informs the computer technician that the images were flashing but it now looks like they are flickering. The computer technician notices some bright spots at the edge of the screen. What is causing this issue? (Choose two)

    A. Check the cable connectors at both ends

    B. Check the display settings

    C. The backlight on the laptop is starting to fail

    D. Reboot the laptop

7. A new TV and video soundbar system has just been set up in a boardroom. The TV is being used to play videos from a presentation laptop. Sound is coming from the laptop and from the TV but the video soundbar is not producing any audio. Which of the following is causing the problem?

    A. The soundbar is not turned on

    B. The soundbar volume is too low

    C. The High-Definition Multimedia Interface-Audio Return Channel (HDMI-ARC) port on the TV is not connected to the soundbar

    D. The video resolution is too low

8. A user has called the help desk as their monitor is showing a purple tinge. Which of the following is most likely causing the problem?

    A. Display burn-in

    B. A faulty graphics card

    C. A bad cable

    D. A burned-out bulb

9. A user complains that the cursor on her screen keeps drifting, and she cannot control it. What should be done to resolve this issue?

   A. Check the video cable

   B. Calibrate the screen

   C. Roll back the graphics driver

   D. Change the screen resolution

10. A computer technician has been called out to a conference room where the projector is intermittently rebooting. What will the computer technician do next? (Choose two)

    A. Change the power cable

    B. Check the vents are dust-free and that there are no obstructions

    C. Check that the projector fan is working properly

    D. Check that the projector can handle the display resolution

11. The plasma screen in a conference room is displaying an image for about 60 seconds after it is shown on the screen. The presenter is using a presentation that is stored on their laptop via an HDMI cable. Which of the following is causing this issue?

    A. Display burn-in

    B. Dead pixels

    C. A faulty cable

    D. The laptop freezing

12. What is the primary purpose of testing the output resolution in a system?

    A. To ensure accurate color representation

    B. To optimize image quality

    C. To verify compatibility with different display devices

    D. To enhance system performance

13. A museum is experiencing issues with the touch-screen functionality on their Windows devices. Which of the following should be checked?

    A. The battery status

    B. The network connection

    C. The display settings

    D. The keyboard settings

5.5 Given a scenario, troubleshoot common issues with mobile devices

1. A computer is experiencing issues during the POST process. What component should be checked?

   A. RAM modules

   B. The CMOS battery

   C. The hard drive

   D. The graphics card

2. A network device is not receiving power through the Ethernet connection. What should be done to resolve the issue?

   A. Check the network cable connections

   B. Restart the network device

   C. Install a Power over Ethernet (PoE) injector

   D. Reset the network settings

3. What could be the cause of a phone becoming excessively hot?

   A. The phone is running resource-intensive apps

   B. The phone is exposed to direct sunlight for a long time

   C. The phone's battery is defective

   D. The phone's operating system needs an update

4. What is the most appropriate action to take if a phone has been exposed to liquid?

   A. Immediately turn on the phone to check whether it is still functioning

   B. Place the phone in a bag of rice for several hours to absorb the moisture

   C. Use a hairdryer on low heat to dry the phone quickly

   D. Take the phone to a professional repair service for assessment and cleaning

5.6 Given a scenario, troubleshoot and resolve printer issues

1. How can a duplex printer help reduce excessive paper usage?

   A. It automatically prints on both sides of the paper

   B. It prints at a slower speed, conserving paper

   C. It uses recycled paper for printing

   D. It has a larger paper tray, reducing the need for frequent refills

2. What could be the potential cause of printed text not sticking to the paper?

    A. The printer is using low-quality ink cartridges

    B. The paper being used is not compatible with the printer

    C. The printer's fuser unit is not functioning properly

    D. The printer's temperature settings are too low

3. What could be the potential cause of a new printer with a duplex unit only being able to print on one side at a time?

    A. The printer's firmware requires an update

    B. The printer's duplex unit is not properly set up

    C. The printer's paper tray is not properly aligned

    D. The printer's ink cartridges are low on ink

4. What could be the potential cause of print quality issues, including marks on the printing paper? (Choose two)

    A. The printer's firmware requires an update

    B. The printer's drum unit is damaged

    C. The printer has dirty feed rollers

    D. The printer's ink cartridges are low on ink

5. When paper fails to feed properly in a printer, what is the most likely cause?

    A. The paper tray is empty

    B. The paper is too thick for the printer

    C. The printer driver needs to be updated

    D. The ink cartridges are low on ink

6. What is the most likely cause of a paper jam in a printer?

    A. The paper tray is empty

    B. The paper is wrinkled or folded

    C. There are obstructions in the paper path

    D. The ink cartridges are low on ink

7. To minimize paper waste and enhance print job control, what measures can be implemented?

    A. Load a large stack of paper into the tray

    B. Print double-sided documents whenever possible

    C. Require a login for print jobs

    D. Avoid using paper trays and feed paper manually

8. How does the failure of air conditioning in the printing environment affect a thermal printer, particularly regarding blank spots or missing text, and how can this issue be resolved?

    A. Causes overheating and damage to the print head; implement adequate ventilation and cooling solutions

    B. Results in increased ink consumption for thermal printing; adjust printer settings for optimized ink usage

    C. Causes blank spots or missing text on thermal paper; clean the print head

    D. Leads to decreased print speed and slower output; upgrade the thermal printer to a higher-performance model

9. Why does a projector power down unexpectedly during operation?

    A. Overheating caused by a dirty air filter

    B. Insufficient power supply to the projector

    C. A malfunctioning lamp in the projector

    D. A loose connection between the projector and power source

10. Why is a printer printing blank receipts?

    A. Empty ink or toner cartridges

    B. Paper feed issues or incorrect paper loading

    C. Overheating of the print head

    D. Outdated printer driver software

11. What type of printer typically uses a ribbon?

    A. An inkjet printer

    B. A laser printer

    C. A thermal printer

    D. A dot matrix printer

12. Why does a dot matrix printer produce documents with missing words?

    A. Worn ribbon in the printer

    B. Paper feed issues or misalignment

    C. Overheating of the print head

    D. Outdated printer driver software

13. Which of the following is the most important factor to prevent the print head from becoming too hot during printing?

    A. Excessive heat can damage the print head and lead to poor print quality

    B. The print head needs to be cold to ensure proper ink flow

    C. Increased temperature enhances the printing speed

    D. Excessive heat can increase the risk of printer malfunctions

14. A user is experiencing gaps in the printed labels from their label printer. What is the MOST likely cause of this issue?

    A. Low ink or toner levels in the printer

    B. Incorrect label alignment or positioning

    C. A paper jam inside the printer

    D. Outdated printer drivers or firmware

15. What could be the cause of a laser printer producing a ghost image on the printed page?

    A. An insufficient fuser temperature

    B. A low toner level

    C. A dirty or damaged imaging drum

    D. A loose connection between the printer and the computer

16. What should you do if you encounter a situation where paper is stuck to the fuser in a newly installed printer?

    A. Use a pair of tweezers or pliers to carefully remove the stuck paper

    B. Turn off the printer, allow it to cool down, and then gently pull the paper out in the direction of the paper path

    C. Ignore the problem and continue printing, as it will likely resolve itself

    D. Contact the printer manufacturer or a technician for assistance

17. A technician is troubleshooting an issue where lines appear down copied pages, but the printed pages sent directly to the copier render as intended. What is the MOST likely cause of this issue?

    A. A clogged printer head

    B. An overheated fuser

    C. Damaged scanning glass

    D. An incompatible toner

18. A laser printer is consistently printing garbled text instead of clear, readable text. What is the MOST likely cause of this issue?

    A. Low ink or toner levels in the printer

    B. Outdated printer drivers or firmware

    C. Damaged printer cables or connections

    D. Incorrect printer settings or font compatibility

19. In a digitization project, which of the following devices would be MOST suitable for capturing electronic images of a large collection of historical handwritten documents?

    A. An NFC device

    B. Flatbed scanner

    C. Digital camera

    D. QR scanner

20. A laser printer consistently prints a line from the top of the page down to the bottom on every sheet. What is the MOST likely cause of this issue?

    A. Low ink or toner levels in the printer

    B. A malfunctioning paper feed mechanism

    C. Outdated printer drivers or firmware

    D. Dust or debris on the imaging drum

21. A printer is producing a grinding noise during printing. What is the MOST likely cause of this issue?

    A. Low ink or toner levels in the printer

    B. A paper jam or obstruction in the printer

    C. Outdated printer drivers or firmware

    D. Network connectivity issues

5.7 Given a scenario, troubleshoot problems with wired and wireless networks

1. You are experiencing issues with your wireless network, and you are unable to select a specific channel for your router. What is the MOST likely cause of this issue?

    A. Interference from nearby devices or networks

    B. Outdated firmware on the wireless router

    C. Incorrect network configuration settings

    D. Insufficient signal strength from the router

2. You have implemented MAC filtering on your wireless network, but some devices are still able to connect without being on the approved list. What is the MOST likely cause of this issue?

    A. Incorrect MAC addresses entered in the filter list

    B. Outdated firmware on the wireless router

    C. Interference from neighboring wireless networks

    D. An incompatible wireless encryption protocol

3. What action should be taken to resolve limited or no connectivity for a wireless client in a network due to an IP address issue?

    A. Release and renew the IP address

    B. Update the network adapter drivers

    C. Adjust the wireless channel

    D. Flush the DNS cache on the computer

4. Which of the following best describes the use of the licensed band in wireless communication?

    A. A reserved frequency spectrum for authorized users

    B. A publicly accessible frequency spectrum

    C. Temporary allocation for experimental purposes

    D. An unlicensed frequency spectrum for general use

5. In a wireless network setup with two routers, what can be done to avoid high latency issues?

    A. Channel bonding

    B. Separate wireless channels, each with its own IP address range

    C. The use of wired connections

    D. Implementation of Quality of Service (QoS)

6. When remotely accessing the company network, which option provides a secure connection to the company LAN?

   A. A Virtual Private Network (VPN)

   B. Enhanced internet speed

   C. Public IP address assignment

   D. Firewall protection

7. What is a possible solution to address a wireless connection that keeps dropping in an office environment?

   A. Relocate the wireless router

   B. Increase the internet bandwidth

   C. Disable other wireless devices

   D. Change the wireless encryption method

8. What is the purpose of using a Wi-Fi analyzer to troubleshoot wireless connectivity issues?

   A. Identifying signal interference sources

   B. Increasing Wi-Fi speed

   C. Changing the Wi-Fi password

   D. Expanding wireless network coverage

9. What could be a potential cause of poor Voice over Internet Protocol (VoIP) quality?

   A. Outdated hardware

   B. Low battery on the device

   C. Insufficient bandwidth

   D. Inadequate microphone sensitivity

Mock Exam

The official CompTIA A+ Core 1 (220-1101) certification exam gives you 90 minutes to complete the test. Hence, it is advisable to set a timer before starting this mock exam to have a good assessment of your preparation level.

1. Which of the following is true about the M.2 form factor?

    A. M.2 supports only the SATA interface

    B. M.2 is exclusively used for graphics cards

    C. M.2 allows faster data transfer rates compared to traditional hard drives

    D. M.2 cannot be used as a boot device

2. What is a characteristic of RAID 5?

    A. Requires a minimum of three drives

    B. Provides the highest level of fault tolerance

    C. Offers increased read performance compared to RAID 0

    D. Requires dedicated parity drives

3. Which of the following flash memory card formats is commonly used in digital cameras?

    A. CompactFlash (CF)

    B. Secure Digital (SD)

    C. Memory Stick (MS)

    D. eXtreme Digital (xD)

4. Which of the following statements about ATX motherboards is true?

    A. ATX motherboards are exclusively designed for Intel processors

    B. ATX motherboards typically have fewer expansion slots compared to microATX

    C. ATX motherboards use the 20-pin ATX power connector

    D. ATX motherboards support dual-channel memory architecture

5. Which of the following is a security feature provided by the UEFI (Unified Extensible Firmware Interface)?

    A. Secure Boot
    B. BIOS password
    C. CMOS clear jumper
    D. Trusted Platform Module (TPM)

6. Which of the following is a primary benefit of using an expansion sound card in a computer?

    A. Increased CPU performance
    B. Enhanced audio quality and capabilities
    C. Improved cooling efficiency
    D. Expanded storage capacity

7. What is the purpose of cooling fans in a computer system?

    A. To increase the display resolution
    B. To provide wireless connectivity
    C. To regulate the temperature of components
    D. To improve sound quality

8. What is the function of a heat sink in a computer?

    A. To amplify audio signals
    B. To provide additional storage space
    C. To dissipate heat from a component
    D. To improve network performance

9. What are motherboard connector headers used for?

    A. To store system configuration settings
    B. To provide additional power to the CPU
    C. To connect peripheral devices
    D. To control the display output

10. What is a key feature of multisocket motherboards?

    A. They support multiple graphics cards simultaneously

    B. They provide advanced overclocking capabilities

    C. They can accommodate multiple CPUs

    D. They offer extensive expandability options

11. What is the main advantage of using PostScript printing?

    A. Faster printing speed

    B. Higher print resolution

    C. Greater color accuracy

    D. Enhanced printer security

12. What is the primary benefit of duplexing in printing?

    A. Reduced paper waste

    B. Faster printing speed

    C. Improved print quality

    D. Increased printer durability

13. What is an important consideration when properly unboxing a device?

    A. Keeping the original packaging materials for future use

    B. Removing all protective films and covers before powering on

    C. Disregarding the instruction manual as it is not necessary

    D. Plugging in the device immediately without inspecting for damage

14. What does adjusting the printer tray settings refer to?

    A. Changing the color settings for printed documents

    B. Configuring the network connectivity of the printer

    C. Adjusting the paper size and type for printing

    D. Aligning the print heads for better print quality

15. What is an important consideration when selecting printer paper for optimal print quality?

    A. Paper weight and thickness

    B. Paper color and texture

    C. Paper brand and manufacturer

    D. Paper price and affordability

16. What does inkjet calibration involve?

    A. Adjusting the ink cartridge settings for optimal performance

    B. Aligning the print heads to ensure precise ink placement

    C. Changing the inkjet printer's connection settings

    D. Cleaning the inkjet carriage to remove debris and dust

17. What is the function of an inkjet carriage belt in a printer?

    A. Transferring ink from the cartridge to the printhead

    B. Controlling the movement of the printhead assembly

    C. Ensuring proper paper feed and alignment

    D. Maintaining optimal ink flow and print quality

18. Which of the following is a primary function of a firewall?

    A. Data encryption

    B. Virus scanning

    C. Network traffic filtering

    D. User authentication

19. What is the main purpose of overclocking a computer component?

    A. To extend the component's lifespan

    B. To reduce power consumption

    C. To increase the component's performance

    D. To improve compatibility with software

20. Which wireless network standard offers the highest data transfer rates?

    A. 802.11a

    B. 802.11b

    C. 802.11g

    D. 802.11ac

21. What is the primary purpose of Network Address Translation (NAT) in networking?

    A. To encrypt network traffic for secure communication

    B. To translate domain names into IP addresses

    C. To assign unique IP addresses to each device on a network

    D. To map private IP addresses to public IP addresses

22. Which port is commonly used for transferring files between a client and a server?

    A. 143

    B. 80

    C. 21

    D. 25

23. Which network protocol is used for secure remote access and secure file transfers?

    A. Secure Shell (SSH)

    B. Simple Network Management Protocol (SNMP)

    C. Post Office Protocol (POP)

    D. Network Time Protocol (NTP)

24. Which network protocol is commonly used for insecure remote command-line access to a server?

    A. Domain Name System (DNS)

    B. HyperText Transfer Protocol (HTTP)

    C. Simple Network Management Protocol (SNMP)

    D. Telnet

25. Which network protocol is primarily used for sending and receiving email messages?

   A. File Transfer Protocol (FTP)

   B. Simple Mail Transfer Protocol (SMTP)

   C. HyperText Transfer Protocol (HTTP)

   D. Post Office Protocol (POP)

26. Which network protocol is responsible for translating domain names into IP addresses?

   A. Domain Name System (DNS)

   B. Dynamic Host Configuration Protocol (DHCP)

   C. HyperText Transfer Protocol (HTTP)

   D. Simple Network Management Protocol (SNMP)

27. Which network protocol is responsible for automatically assigning IP addresses to devices on a network?

   A. Simple Network Management Protocol (SNMP)

   B. Domain Name System (DNS)

   C. HyperText Transfer Protocol (HTTP)

   D. Dynamic Host Configuration Protocol (DHCP)

28. Which feature allows mobile devices to determine their geographic location?

   A. Global Positioning System (GPS)

   B. Wi-Fi connectivity

   C. Bluetooth technology

   D. Near-Field Communication (NFC)

29. Which technology allows cellular networks to estimate the location of a mobile device?

   A. Wi-Fi positioning

   B. Cellular tower triangulation

   C. Bluetooth proximity detection

   D. GPS satellite tracking

30. What is the primary purpose of Mobile Device Management (MDM) and Mobile Application Management (MAM) solutions?

    A. To encrypt mobile device communications

    B. To secure mobile devices against physical theft

    C. To manage and control mobile device configurations and applications

    D. To provide remote wipe functionality for lost devices

31. Which protocol is commonly used for corporate email configuration on mobile devices?

    A. POP3 (Post Office Protocol version 3)

    B. IMAP (Internet Message Access Protocol)

    C. SMTP (Simple Mail Transfer Protocol)

    D. LDAP (Lightweight Directory Access Protocol)

32. What is the primary purpose of two-factor authentication (2FA)?

    A. To encrypt data during transmission

    B. To provide secure physical access to devices

    C. To verify the identity of users with an additional authentication factor

    D. To prevent unauthorized access to corporate applications

33. What is the purpose of the remote wipe feature on a stolen mobile phone?

    A. To physically retrieve the stolen device

    B. To track the location of the stolen device

    C. To delete all data on the stolen device remotely

    D. To disable the stolen device's network connectivity

34. What is the purpose of enabling Bluetooth on a device?

    A. To establish a wireless internet connection

    B. To pair and connect with other Bluetooth devices

    C. To enable GPS navigation

    D. To increase battery life

35. What action needs to be taken to enable pairing on a Bluetooth device?

   A. Pressing a specific button on the device

   B. Installing Bluetooth drivers

   C. Connecting the device to a power source

   D. Updating the device's operating system

36. What does the process of finding a device for pairing in Bluetooth involve?

   A. Scanning for nearby Bluetooth devices

   B. Connecting to a Wi-Fi network

   C. Syncing data between devices

   D. Enabling location services

37. What action should be taken to enable or disable the wireless/cellular data network on a mobile device?

   A. Access the device's settings and toggle the data network option

   B. Contact the mobile service provider for activation or deactivation

   C. Restart the device to automatically enable or disable the data network

   D. Update the device's operating system to enable or disable data connectivity

38. Which two wireless/cellular technology standards are commonly used for voice and data communication?

   A. 3G and 4G

   B. GSM and CDMA

   C. Bluetooth and Wi-Fi

   D. LTE and WiMAX

39. What does the hotspot feature on a mobile device allow you to do?

   A. Create a secure wireless network for nearby devices to connect

   B. Enable high-speed data connectivity in remote areas

   C. Share the device's internet connection with other devices

   D. Connect to public Wi-Fi networks automatically

40. What is the purpose of Preferred Roaming List (PRL) updates on a mobile device?

   A. To enable international roaming capabilities

   B. To update the device's network security protocols

   C. To improve the device's call and data connection quality

   D. To optimize the device's battery usage during roaming

41. Which type of IP address is assigned to devices that are connected to the internet?

   A. Private addresses

   B. Loopback addresses

   C. Reserved addresses

   D. Public addresses

42. What is the maximum data transfer rate supported by USB 2.0?

   A. 480 Mbps

   B. 1 Gbps

   C. 5 Gbps

   D. 10 Gbps

43. What is the maximum data transfer rate supported by USB 3.0?

   A. 480 Mbps

   B. 1 Gbps

   C. 5 Gbps

   D. 10 Gbps

44. Which type of network is typically confined to a small geographic area, such as an office building or campus?

   A. Local Area Network (LAN)

   B. Wide Area Network (WAN)

   C. Personal Area Network (PAN)

   D. Metropolitan Area Network (MAN)

45. Which type of network spans a large geographical area and connects multiple LANs?

    A. Local Area Network (LAN)

    B. Wide Area Network (WAN)

    C. Personal Area Network (PAN)

    D. Metropolitan Area Network (MAN)

46. What is the maximum data transfer rate typically supported by Fast Ethernet (100BASE-TX) technology?

    A. 10 Mbps

    B. 100 Mbps

    C. 1 Gbps

    D. 10 Gbps

47. Which Ethernet standard supports a maximum data transfer rate of 10 gigabits per second (Gbps)?

    A. 10BASE-T

    B. 100BASE-TX

    C. Gigabit Ethernet (1000BASE-T)

    D. 10 Gigabit Ethernet (10GBASE-T)

48. What is the maximum data transfer rate supported by the Cat 5 cable?

    A. 10 Mbps

    B. 100 Mbps

    C. 1 Gbps

    D. 10 Gbps

49. Which range of IP addresses is reserved for use as private IP addresses within internal networks?

    A. 10.0.0.0 – 10.255.255.255

    B. 179.16.0.0 – 179.30.255.255

    C. 212.16.0.0 – 212.16.255.255

    D. 169.254.0.0 – 169.254.255.255

50. What is the purpose of Automatic Private IP Addressing (APIPA) in a network?

   A. To assign globally routable IP addresses to devices in a private network

   B. To automatically assign public IP addresses to devices in a network

   C. To provide temporary IP addresses when a DHCP server is unavailable

   D. To enable communication between devices in different private networks

Solutions

Chapter 1: Mobile Devices

1.1 Given a scenario, install and configure laptop hardware and components

1. The correct answer is **A**. The biometric reader should be set up on each laptop or desktop for only the user of that device. In the accounts department, only one person should have access to each device. All other answers are incorrect. Some users in accounts may deal with more sensitive data, and it is therefore inadvisable to give everyone access to their laptop/desktop. Employees from other departments should not be permitted access to any account's devices. Guests are people from other companies and should not be given access to any company resources.

2. The correct answer is **B**. RAM is volatile, and you will need to wear an electrostatic discharge strap to protect the RAM against any static electricity. All other answers are incorrect. DDR RAM is for desktops, and SODIMMs are used by laptops. You would only check the power voltage if you had power problems. Operating system updates have no relationship to RAM upgrades.

3. The correct answer is **D**. When the laptop is used at work, the power lead will likely be plugged into the power socket and draw power from the mains. Therefore, the most likely source of the problem in this scenario is the battery. All other answers are incorrect. If the device works correctly when plugged into the mains, the problem is unlikely to be the power adapter. If the operating system is corrupt, the laptop will still power up but display a blue screen of death. If the system fan is used as a cooling device aiding airflow, its failure would cause the computer to overheat and then crash, not prevent it from booting up.

4. The correct answer is **D**. A Small Outline Dual In-Line Memory Module (SODIMM) is smaller and thinner so that it fits into a laptop that has restricted space. All other answers are incorrect. A Dual In-Line Memory Module (DIMM) is normally known as a RAM stick and is about double the size of a SODIMM, and is used for desktop computers, workstations, and servers. Double Data Rate 3 (DDR3) RAM is larger than a SODIMM commonly used in computers, though you can now get SODIMM versions. Synchronous Dynamic Random Access Memory (SDRAM) is larger than a SODIMM and is used in desktop computers.

5. The correct answers are **B**, **C**, **D**, and **E**. When installing a Solid-State Drive (SSD) into a laptop, you must first shut the system down, then disconnect the power cable and remove the battery. You must then ground yourself by wearing an Electrostatic Discharge (ESD) wrist strap to protect the components against the static electricity in your body. The remaining answer choice is incorrect. Clearing your desk would be nice, but it is not a safety precaution.

6. The correct answers are **B** and **C**. The iPhone 10 uses Touch ID, and iPhone 11 uses Face ID. All other answers are incorrect. iPhones cannot use fingerprint or vein ID, the latter of which is another name for a palm scan.

7. The correct answer is **C**. When the battery has come to the end of its life, it will not fully charge nor retain charge for very long. It will also have a tendency to overheat. All other answers are incorrect. The digitizer is the glass on the front of the phone that is used by the touchscreen and would not make the phone hot, even if it were broken. If the cable were faulty, there would be no charge, but the phone would not be hot either. When an iPhone battery is set to low power mode, less power is used and the phone should therefore be cooler.

8. The correct answer is **B**. A DHCP client will only get an Automatic Private IP Address (APIPA) if it cannot obtain an IP address from the DHCP server. This could be because of network issues contacting the DHCP server or because the server has run out of IP addresses. All other answers are incorrect. DNS is used for hostname-to-IP-address name resolution. NETBIOS is a legacy Microsoft name resolution protocol. If they were using a static IP address, then DHCP Enabled would be set to No.

9. All answer choices are correct. The first stage is to make a full backup of the HDD, just in case anything goes wrong. You'll thereafter remove any redundant data that you are not going to migrate, resize the data partition so it is less than the size of the SSD, clone the old HDD partition, shut down the laptop and remove the old HDD, install and initialize the SSD, and finally, restore the cloned data onto the SSD.

10. The correct answer is **D**. A 13.56-MHz frequency is used by RFID applications. This includes Near-Field Communication (NFC), which is a scanner type used in door access and card payment systems. All other answers are incorrect. Biometrics would not use the phone as an interface. You would simply use your fingerprint or facial recognition to gain access. Certificates are used for encryption and not as an access control. Open Authentication (OAuth) is used for internet-based authentication only.

11. The correct answer is **B**. Most Solid-State Drives (SSDs) come in a 2.5-inch standard form factor. All other answers are incorrect. 3.5 inches is the size of a converter to place an SSD into a computer. 5.25 and 8 inches were the sizes of the first floppy disks.

12. The correct answer is **C**. He should first confirm the power rating of the charger, which is most likely too low to charge the phone and therefore the most probable cause of the issue. All other answers are incorrect. Deleting unwanted apps will reduce resources used by the phone but will not prevent it from charging. Putting the phone back to its factory setting will not fix a power issue. Setting the battery to low power mode will use less battery once the phone has been charged but will do nothing to resolve the current problem.

13. The correct answers are **A** and **D**. The easiest of the available options is a Bluetooth-enabled keyboard to connect to an Android tablet. You can also use a USB-C connector, which you would then connect to either DVI or, preferably, HDMI. All other answers are incorrect. No tablet has an Ethernet connection as these devices are too thin. Lightning cables are used only by Apple phones and tablets.

14. The correct answer is **A**. Near-Field Communication (NFC) is commonly used for card payments. All other answers are incorrect. Tethering is the process of creating a personal hotspot. A digitizer provides touchscreen technology. Dedicated VPN software creates a VPN.

1.2 Compare and contrast the display components of mobile devices

1. The correct answer is **D**. The digitizer is a piece of glass that enables touchscreen technology. All other answers are incorrect. The inverter converts DC to AC power. Vertical Alignment (VA) supports a contrast ratio of 2000:1. The backlight controls the brightness of an LCD monitor.

2. The correct answer is **D**. The gyroscope is used by the phone to rotate the screen as you twist your phone around. All other answers are incorrect. The bezel is the border between the phone's frames and the screen. The digitizer is a layer of glass that enables touchscreen functionality. The accelerometer tracks the motion of the phone and adjusts the screen size.

3. The correct answer is **C**. Since the webcam is not showing an image, it is likely to be a setup issue. In this case, reinstalling the webcam is the best solution. All other answers are incorrect. Rebooting the computer will not resolve an image issue. Purchasing a new webcam is unnecessary. Plugging the webcam into another port is unlikely to resolve an image issue.

4. The correct answer is **C**. An inverter converts DC power to AC power. All other answers are incorrect. An inverter does not convert AC to DC power. A digitizer is a piece of glass that provides touchscreen functionality. A backlight increases readability in low-light conditions.

5. The correct answer is **A**. Twisted Nematic (TN) displays use crystals that twist or untwist depending on the voltage level. It supports fast response time in relation to other TFT displays. All other answers are incorrect. Modern IPS displays have similar response times to TN, but the crystals rotate rather than twist. VA panels are prone to blurring and ghosting. A Cathode Ray Tube (CRT) has a display that is prone to screen burn-in and ghosting due to non-uniform use of the screen.

6. The correct answer is **C**. In Windows, if the microphone is not working properly, you should go to Privacy, select Microphone, then ensure the Allow apps to access your microphone feature is turned on. All other answers are incorrect. Rebooting the laptop is unlikely to resolve the issue. Getting an up-to-date driver is unlikely to resolve the issue if you have not enabled access for apps to the microphone. Purchasing additional voice recognition software will not resolve the issue if voice recognition is not enabled in the privacy settings.

7. The correct answer is **C**. An LCD monitor gets its brightness from a backlight, so if it fails, the screen may be very dim or even black. All other answers are incorrect. The backlight failing has no relationship to the brightness settings. You can have the brightness set to its highest setting, but if the backlight is malfunctioning, the screen will still be dim. A digitizer is used in touchscreen technology, and a legacy LCD monitor will not be touchscreen. If the VGA cable were broken, the screen would be black.

8. The correct answer is **D**. The digitizer is a thin layer of glass that converts analog touch into digital signals, and in this scenario, the most likely reason for the black areas is that the digitizer is broken. All other answers are incorrect. The Liquid Contact Indicators (LCIs) on an iPhone are normally white or silver, and if the phone has suffered water damage, these will be red. Look at the side of the phone with a lighted magnifying glass to view this. Inverters are used by older laptops to convert DC power from the motherboard to AC power. If the brightness of the phone were too low, it would be uniform across the entire screen and would not appear as dark patches.

9. The correct answer is **D**. In-Plane Switching (IPS) uses crystals that rotate rather than twist. This means that it produces better color definition with a wider range of viewing angles, making it suitable for both gaming and graphic design. All other answers are incorrect. LEDs can be used for low-budget gaming but not for graphic design. LCDs deliver less color accuracy than LED displays, which makes them a poor choice. CRTs are a legacy display technology and are not suitable for either gaming or graphic design.

10. The correct answer is **B**. Vertical Alignment (VA) uses crystals that tilt rather than twist or rotate and supports a wider color gamut and a contrast ratio of 2000:1 or 3000:1. However, the viewing angles are not as good as In-Plane Switching (IPS), making it more prone to blurring and ghosting. All other answers are incorrect. OLED could be described as having an infinite contrast ratio and can support 1,000,000:1. IPS can only support a contrast ratio of up to 1200:1. VGA has an aspect ratio of 4:3.

11. The correct answer is **C**. In an Organic Light-Emitting Diode (OLED) display, each pixel is produced by a separate LED. This screen therefore does not require a separate backlight. OLEDs are used in modern TVs, smartphones, monitors, and tablets. All other answers are incorrect. A Cathode Ray Tube (CRT) is a legacy display and uses a backlight. Liquid Crystal Displays (LCDs) use a fluorescent backlight. Light-Emitting Diode (LED) displays also use various backlight configurations.

12. The correct answer is **D**. When users have connected dual monitors and there is no image, they will need to adjust the display settings by going to Settings, Home, Display, Multiple Displays, and then selecting Extend these displays. This will enable dual monitors. All other answers are incorrect. If they choose the Duplicate these displays option, the image will be the same on both screens. They cannot create a dual-monitor setup using the Projecting to this PC option.

13. The correct answers are **A** and **D**. The iPhone must be within 10 meters of the speaker, and Bluetooth must be enabled in user Settings. All other answers are incorrect. There is no Bluetooth option under General settings, and 20 meters is out of the range of Bluetooth devices.

14. The correct answer is **C**. The wireless antenna is normally located on the bezel on the top of the laptop. All other answers are incorrect. There are no interface cards on the front or the rear of a laptop; they are normally on the sides. If the wireless antenna were on the base, there would be no signal.

15. The correct answer is **A**. The digitizer is a piece of glass that sits over the phone screen and enables touchscreen functionality. When you can see the icons perfectly but cannot open them, this most likely means that the digitizer is broken and will need to be replaced. All other answers are incorrect. If there was no power, the screen would be black. A broken CPU would mean that each app would respond but would be much slower than normal. "All of the above" is not the correct solution as some answers are incompatible.

16. The correct answers are **B** and **C**. The touchpad (sometimes known as the trackpad) can be used instead of a mouse. If it is unresponsive, the first step is to remove an external mouse. If that does not work, then you need a driver update. All other answers are incorrect. Rebooting the laptop will not resolve this issue. A gyroscope is used by phones and tablets to rotate their screens when you change the orientation of the device.

1.3 Given a scenario, set up and configure accessories and ports of mobile devices

1. The correct answer is **D**. The charger for iPhone 10 uses a Lightning cable. All other answers are incorrect. USB-A is used by computers, TVs, and gaming consoles. USB-B is used by printers, and USB-C is used by Android phones and most other new devices, such as game controllers and earbud cases.

2. The correct answers are **A** and **C**. A legacy laptop will not have a USB 3.0 port. It could also be that the USB slot is the wrong form factor. All other answers are incorrect. It is very unlikely that the USB drive being upside down is the source of the problem, as any user would try it both ways around, thereby easily resolving the issue. It is unlikely that damage has been caused to the end of a USB drive as it is very robust. It would be more likely to be the case that is damaged.

3. The correct answer is **B**. The Samsung Galaxy uses a USB-C connector. All other answers are incorrect. No phones use a normal USB connector. Micro USBs are used for small devices such as power banks, headphones, and gaming controllers. Mini USB ports were used to transfer data from early smartphones and PDAs.

4. The correct answer is **A**. When a cable cannot be fully inserted into a charging port, the most likely reason is a build-up of lint or another foreign object that is lodged in the port. The best way to remove the lint is to give it a good blast of compressed air. All other answers are incorrect. You should not blow into the port as your breath contains moisture that could damage the electrical components. You should never use WD-40 as it is a liquid and spraying electrical components is an electrical hazard. When it dries it leaves an oily residue. You could also use a toothpick for this job, but using a metal object such as a pin or needle risks causing an electrical short circuit that could damage the phone.

5.   The correct answers are **B** and **C**. Before using any Bluetooth product, you must first enable Bluetooth on the phone, then pair both devices. All other answers are incorrect. There is no need to install drivers on a smartphone that has built-in Bluetooth capability. Until the devices are paired, any music you play will come through the phone speakers and not the earbuds.

6.   The correct answers are **A**, **D**, and **E**. A docking station is a sophisticated port replicator and, when combined with DisplayPort, can provide keyboard and mouse, speaker, and dual-monitor functionality. All other answers are incorrect. Wi-Fi normally comes built in, but if the laptop is older, you may need to purchase a Wi-Fi card. Laptops usually come with Ethernet ports, but for older models, you will need to purchase a network card.

7.   The correct answer is **C**. Using a smartphone to create a personal hotspot is the fastest way to get internet access on their laptop. All other answers are incorrect. Traveling 10 miles might mean missing the conference call due to traffic and the user would be overheard by other Starbucks customers even if they did make it in time. Connecting an Ethernet cable directly to a wireless router that has no connectivity is not a solution. Rebooting the wireless router is not going to obtain an internet connection.

8.   The correct answer is **B**. Port replicators can be plugged into the back of a laptop to give the user a variety of additional ports. All other answers are incorrect. A KVM switch is used for the keyboard, mouse, and monitor when there are multiple monitors or computers attached. A dual monitor will only give you a second monitor; it will not fulfill the other requirements. A hub is an internal device that is used to connect multiple computers.

9.   The correct answers are **A**, **C**, and **D**. When you are having problems with the touchscreen, and it shows any erratic behavior, the first thing you should do is check that the screen is not damaged. Then, check that it is clean. After that, you should recalibrate the screen. The remaining answer is incorrect. The touch pen battery life has nothing to do with erratic cursor behavior. If the battery were running low, the touch pen would simply become unresponsive.

10. The correct answer is **C**. The micro USB connection was replaced by the USB-C cable. All other answers are incorrect. Serial cables are legacy cables that used an RS232 port. Lightning cables are used by Apple devices only. Parallel cables are old cables used by printers and have since been replaced by USB.

11. The correct answer is **C**. The iPhone 14 uses a USB-C charger. All other answers are incorrect. The charger for iPhone 11 uses a Lightning cable, while iPhone 12 and 13 models come with a Lightning-to-USB-C connector. USB-A is used by computers, TV, and gaming consoles. USB-B is used by printers, and USB-C is used by Android phones and most new devices, such as game controllers and earbud cases.

12. The correct answer is **D**. Serial devices that use the nine-pin RS-232 hardware port include legacy mice, printers, and modems. All other answers are incorrect. RJ45 is used by Ethernet cables. RJ11 was used to connect a modem to a telephone line. Parallel connections are used by legacy printers.

13. The correct answers are **A** and **C**. Web cameras can only provide input to one type of software at a time. If the webcam privacy setting is not set to Allow apps to access this camera, then the webcam will not work. All other answers are incorrect. It is unlikely that plugging the webcam into another port will resolve the issue as it worked yesterday. Purchasing another webcam will not resolve the issue of software clashes or enable the camera setting to allow apps to use the camera.

14. The correct answer is **B**. Windows devices have features such as sensitivity and touch mode for touchscreens. You can adjust the touchscreen settings and calibrate the screen under the computer settings. All other answers are incorrect. When setting up the touchscreen, a digitizer is installed. At the time of this installation, the technician must ensure that there are no air bubbles. However, as the screen was working previously (i.e., after its initial installation), air bubbles beneath the glass are not likely to be the current problem. The display settings affect the screen, not the touchscreen itself. A touchscreen only needs between 0.1 and 2 watts; it is a very low-power aspect of the device.

15. The correct answer is **C**. When a webcam stops functioning, the first thing to try is to unplug it and then plug it back in. If that fails to work, then you should uninstall it completely and reinstall the webcam software and any latest updates from the manufacturer's website. All other answers are incorrect. When an update is applied to an operating system, it is likely that the computer has already been rebooted as part of the update, so doing so again is unlikely to help. It is most likely that there is nothing wrong with the webcam, and the user may not have enough time to go to the shops, make a purchase, and set it up before the Zoom conference commences. There is no need to update the operating system as this has already been done and is the root cause of this issue.

16. The correct answer is **C**. NFC is used for card payment types where the card must be within four inches of the reader and so would be the source of the problem described. All other answers are incorrect. Bluetooth is too insecure for financial transactions. Wireless is not used by contactless cards. Infrared requires a line of sight between two devices and has no security; therefore, it is not used for financial transactions.

17. The correct answers are **B**, **C**, and **E**. When a cell phone gets hot, it may be due to excessive use, such as being used as a Wi-Fi hotspot for a long time. Phones also overheat when the battery is nearing the end of its lifespan, at which point it also fails to charge fully and can lose charge very quickly. Having too many applications open at the same time forces the CPU to work harder than normal and, especially in the case of outdated applications, can also increase the phone's temperature. All other answers are incorrect. A cracked screen does not make the phone hot but may prevent the screen from responding. A cheap charging cable will prevent the phone's battery from being charged.

18. The correct answer is **A**. Apple introduced the reversible Lightning cable in 2012 to replace the Apple 30-pin connector. All other answers are incorrect. 20-pin and 25-pin connectors do not exist. Most of Android phones use the USB-C connector.

1.4 Given a scenario, configure basic mobile-device network connectivity and application support

1. The correct answer is **B**. Most companies have a data cap on their mobile devices and wireless routers that need to be topped up once the limit has been reached. All other answers are incorrect. Network coverage must be available in the area as the salesperson was able to watch a movie online the previous evening. MDM solutions test updates prior to releasing them. Companies are highly unlikely to miss mobile phone payments as they are critical to business operations.

2. The correct answer is **B**. A password is "something you know" and a fingerprint is "something you are". This is an example of two-factor authentication. All other answers are incorrect. A retina and fingerprint are both "something you are", a password and PIN are both "something you know", and gait and swiping a card are both "something you do".

3. The correct answer is A. If a SIM card is not installed in a new smartphone, the user will not be able to make any calls or get access to mobile data. All other answers are incorrect. You cannot turn on mobile data without a SIM card. The film protecting the screen does not affect call functionality or mobile data. Activating Bluetooth does not affect calls or mobile data.

4. The correct answer is **B**. The easiest way to pair an Apple Watch with an iPhone is to use the Apple Watch app. This is done by aligning the watch face with your phone camera, just as you would scan a QR code. All other answers are incorrect. Although you can manually set up pairing by entering a six-digit passcode, it is not the easiest method. You cannot pair devices manually using a four-digit passcode; it needs to be six digits. The four-digit code is only used to access the Apple Watch itself.

5. The correct answer is **C**. When a calendar application is not updating, it is normally down to the password not being updated. Updating the corporate password should resolve the issue. All other answers are incorrect. The remaining battery has no impact on the calendar application. Rebooting the phone will not have any impact on the phone app. Remotely wiping the phone will not help in this scenario as doing so will revert the device to its factory settings.

6. The correct answer is **B**. A Global System for Mobile Communication-based phone has a removable SIM that can be inserted into another handset with the same network provider. All other answers are incorrect. Global System for Mobile Communication can work with cellular, wireless, and satellite communications, so all other answers that use the word "only" are false.

7. The correct answer is **C**. MDM solutions allow you to enforce policies and send updates to smartphones. Remotely wiping devices will revert them to factory settings. All other answers are incorrect. WPA2 PSK means connecting to a wireless network using a password. Disabling Bluetooth will only prevent Bluetooth devices from being used. Using a VPN on company phones only secures a remote session from the phone. It does not prevent access to the local data on the phone.

8. The correct answers are **B** and **C**. MAM solutions are used to set policies for apps that can process corporate data and prevent the transfer of corporate data to personal devices. All other answers are incorrect. Mobile Device Management (MDM) is responsible for patching mobile devices and remotely wiping them when they are lost or stolen to prevent data compromise.

9. The correct answer is **B**. Samsung Galaxy users use Google Drive as their backup location. All other answers are incorrect. Gmail is the Google email application. Knox containers are used by Samsung to separate personal and business data on their phones. Office 365 is a Microsoft product.

10. The correct answer is **D**. When a user downloads and installs an app from the Apple App Store, they need their Apple ID and password. If the installation fails, they will need to reset the password. All other answers are incorrect. A Hotmail account is used to access Microsoft products. A Gmail account is used to access Google products. The iPhone passcode is used to access the iPhone itself.

11. The correct answer is **D**. Satellite communication devices connect to satellites above the earth and can communicate in areas where no cell phone masts exist. All other answers are incorrect. Digital Subscriber Line (DSL) requires the use of a splitter to enable phone and internet to be used at the same time. A hotspot connects to a wireless or cellular provider and cannot be used in this case.

12. The correct answer is **C**. If the weather app is left running constantly, it will drain the iPhone battery. They need to both turn off severe weather notifications and modify the location permissions so that they can manually enter the location for which they want to get results. All other answers are incorrect. The location services While Using Your App will still drain the battery. Turning off location services does not affect the weather app. It merely prevents the user from getting notifications when they enter a different country. A local wireless network connection merely provides internet and would not drain the battery. Purchasing a new battery will not resolve this issue.

13. The correct answer is **B**. When the phone is set to power conservation mode, the battery will only charge 50-60%. Smartphones may enter low power mode if the battery is being drained too quickly, and GPS will not work when the phone is in low power mode. Switching this off would correct the issue. All other answers are incorrect. Enabling Bluetooth only allows Bluetooth devices to connect to the phone. Cleaning the touchscreen does not affect GPS. GPS does not use Wi-Fi settings.

14. The correct answer is **C**. If the agent turns off location services, they will prevent the phone's GPS location from being advertised. All other answers are incorrect. You cannot set location services to pause, nor can you delete them.

15. The correct answer is **D**. Your iPhone is backed up to iCloud. All other answers are incorrect. Microsoft uses Office 365, and Google uses Google Drive. Apple uses neither. Boot Camp is an Apple product, but its purpose is to host third-party operating systems.

16. The correct answer is **A**. In Windows 10, the tile turns blue when Bluetooth is switched on. All other answers are incorrect. The tile is gray when it is switched off. The Bluetooth tile will never appear white or green in Windows 10.

17. The correct answer is **D**. Data Loss Prevention (DLP) prevents someone from sending an email containing PII and sensitive information. It blocks data if it finds a pattern match. All other answers are incorrect. A legal hold prevents users from deleting emails from a mailbox. MailTips warn you of events such as a large distribution group being chosen prior to dispatching an email. A firewall is used to block traffic coming into or going out of your company's networks.

18. The correct answer is **C**. GSM phones have removable SIM cards that can be used in another handset from the same provider, whereas CDMA phones have no SIM cards as the provider has a built-in handset. All other options are incorrect.

19. The correct answer is **B**. The Preferred Roaming List (PRL) is a database held on your mobile telephone. This is used when your phone connects to the tower. The salesperson will need to install a PRL update to enable roaming data on their smartphone. All other answers are incorrect. A firmware update will not update the PRL database on your phone. Turning on location services just advertises the location of your phone. Restarting the smartphone will not work in this situation.

20. The correct answer is **C**. The user will need to go to Settings, then Mobile Data, to enable a 4G data connection. All other answers are incorrect. Wi-Fi calling only allows you to communicate from remote locations as long are there is an internet connection over Wi-Fi.

21. The correct answers are **A**, **C**, **D**, and **E**. Following a 14-day free trial, a Google Workspace subscription starts at $5.75 per user and allows access to many applications, at least 30 GB of storage, and video meetings with up to 100 users. All other answers are incorrect. You cannot create virtual machines, and a live.com email address is for Microsoft products.

22. The correct answer is **B**. A legal hold means that a mailbox has no mailbox limit, and any deleted emails are retained in a purges folder. This prevents a user under investigation from deleting emails. All other answers are incorrect. If they set a backup at a certain time each day, they will not capture any emails that have been removed from the deleted items folder. A forensic toolkit is used to extract data from a computer and will not be able to extract emails that have been deleted from the deleted items container. Chain of custody refers to the bagging, tagging, and signing over of evidence to anyone handling the data to prove to the judge that it is the original evidence.

23. The correct answers are **B**, **C**, and **D**. If you are wearing a headset, go into Zoom, then Audio Settings | Microphone | Test mic. When testing a Bluetooth connection, if you are wearing earbuds, then go to your phone and play some music. If you hear music, then you are connected. If you are wearing a headset, you can go into Zoom, and under Audio Settings, you can go to Speaker | Test speaker. All other answers are incorrect. There are no options under Video Settings to test speakers or microphones as it deals only with the camera and video. A Bluetooth connection is only shown in blue when you are using a Windows 10 laptop and not earbuds.

Chapter 2: Networking

2.1 Compare and contrast TCP and UDP ports, protocols, and their purposes

1. The correct answer is **B**. Secure Shell (SSH) is used for secure remote access. All other answers are incorrect. Telnet provides unsecure remote access, RDP uses port 3389 and is a secure remote access protocol that can only be used to connect to Microsoft desktops/servers, and SNMP 161 is unsecure and provides status and reports on network devices.

2. The correct answer is **B**. Hypertext Protocol Secure (HTTPS) is used when establishing a secure session on a web server. All other answers are incorrect. TFTP is unsecure and is used to transfer configuration files. HTTP is used to make an unsecure session on a web server. SSH is used for secure remote access.

3. The correct answer is **A**. Post Office Protocol (POP) is a legacy mail client that stores emails locally and uses port 110. All other answers are incorrect. IMAP is a mail client that provides diaries and calendars, allows you to create multiple folders, has a permanent connection to the mail server, and uses TCP port 143; SMTP is used to transfer email between mail servers and uses TCP port 25.

4. The correct answer is **C**. Server Message Block (SMB) uses port 445 for file and print sharing in a Windows environment. However, it is internal only and cannot be used on the internet. All other answers are incorrect. NETBIOS (ports 137-139) is used for legacy name registration and resolution by Microsoft. 67/68 are used by DHCP to automatically assign IP addresses. 389 is used by LDAP that is used to manage directory services by querying and updating X500 directory objects.

5. The correct answer is **B**. Port 995 is the standard port used by Secure Post Office Protocol (SPOP). All other answers are incorrect. Unsecure POP uses 110. Secure IMAP uses 993. Unsecure IMAP uses 143.

6. The correct answer is **C**. User Datagram Protocol (UDP) is connectionless and can be used to stream video and audio. All other answers are incorrect. TCP is connection-orientated and far too slow for audio or streaming video. RDP is used for secure remote access to Windows servers/desktops. TFTP is a connectionless fast transfer of data. Normally, it is used by network devices to obtain configuration files.

7. The correct answer is **D**. Simple Network Management Protocol (SNMP) v3 is secure and uses UDP port 162. All other answers are incorrect. SNMP uses UDP port 161 but is insecure. Port 389 is used by LDAP to create, manage, and search directory services. POP (the unsecure mail client) uses TCP port 110.

8. The correct answer is **B**. File Transfer Protocol (FTP) port 21 is unsecure and transfers data in clear text. All other answers are incorrect. TFTP is a UDP version of FTP. SSH is a secure method of remote administration. FTPS is a secure version of FTP.

9. The correct answers are **B** and **D**. Hypertext Transfer Protocol (HTTP) uses port 80 and Hypertext Transfer Protocol Secure (HTTPS) uses port 443. All other answers are incorrect. Port 23 is used by Telnet. Port 110 is used by POP. Port 445 is used by SMB.

10. The correct answer is **D**. The correct sequence for the Transmission Control Protocol (TCP) three-way handshake is SYN, then SYN-ACK, and, finally, ACK. The sequences in all the other answers are incorrect.

11. The correct answer is **D**. Simple Mail Transfer Protocol (SMTP) uses port 25. All other answers are incorrect. FTP uses port 21. SFTP, SSH, and SCP all use port 22. Telnet uses port 23.

12. The correct answer is **A**. Port 993 is the standard port used by secure Internet Mail Access Protocol (IMAP). All other answers are incorrect. Unsecure POP uses 110. Secure POP uses 995. Unsecure IMAP uses 143.

13. The correct answer is **C**. Telnet is an insecure remote access protocol. All other answers are incorrect. SSL is an encryption-based protocol designed for securing connections between web clients and servers. SSH is a secure remote access protocol than can replace Telnet. RDP is a secure access protocol for Windows operating systems.

2.2 Compare and contrast common networking hardware

1. The correct answers are **B** and **C**. The back of the patch panel is where wires are terminated at the IDC using a punch-down tool, and the front has prewired RJ45 ports. All other answers are false.

2. The correct answer is **C**. An SDN allows the rapid provisioning and deprovisioning of networks in a virtual environment. All other answers are incorrect. A WAN is a network over a large geographical area. A LAN is a network that is secure and doesn't extend beyond close proximity, for example, a building or even just a single floor of the building. A SAN comprises fast redundant disks.

3. The correct answer is **D**. A UTM solution can perform multiple security functions. All other answers are incorrect. A stateless firewall can only perform basic packet filtering. A host-based firewall can only protect a desktop or laptop, blocking and allowing certain types of traffic. A stateful firewall can provide deep inspection of traffic to assess the verbs in use. For example, in HTTP traffic, the GET verb can be allowed while the PUT or POST verbs can be blocked.

4. The correct answer is **B**. The ONT converts optical signals to electrical signals. All other answers are incorrect. FTTC is where a telecom provider runs fiber cables to multiple customers. ONT does not convert electrical signals to optical signals. The reverse is true. An optical line terminal (OLT) is located in a street cabinet, and the ONT is on the customer's premises.

5. The correct answer is **A**. Power over Ethernet (POE) allows a device to pull its power from the switch. All other answers are incorrect. Thunderbolt can be used as a display interface, similar to HDMI or a display port. A managed switch is an enterprise switch that has 28 or 48 ports and can be configured by a web or command-line interface. A shielded twisted pair cable has the wires wrapped in foil for more protection and to limit EMI.

6. The correct answer is **A**. A broadcast domain refers to the number of people that you can broadcast to. If you create a Virtual Local Area Network (VLAN) on a managed switch, you can reduce its size. All other answers are incorrect. A load balancer sends an incoming client request to the least utilized of a number of web servers performing the same function. A router joins multiple networks together. A hub is a slow device that connects multiple hosts together.

7. The correct answer is **A**. A Storage Area Network (SAN) is a set of fast redundant disks used by virtual servers for storage to host the server's virtual machines. All other answers are incorrect. A PAN is a personal area network normally used by Bluetooth devices and smartphones. A cluster uses a quorum disk that is shared by two servers, one of which is active and the other passive and waiting for the active server to fail. RAID 0 is a setup involving an array of disks as a stripe set for faster reads. However, if one disk fails, then it takes down the whole RAID 0 configuration. It does not provide fault tolerance or redundancy.

8. The correct answer is **C**. Installing power injectors allows you to connect your POE device to a non-POE switch. All other answers are incorrect. A UPS is used to allow a server to shut down gracefully following a complete loss of power. A generator is an alternative power source following a complete loss of power. The purchase of two POE-capable switches is not cost effective.

9. The correct answer is **D**. An unmanaged switch is taken out of the box and plugged in. All other answers are incorrect. A managed switch is an enterprise switch that has 28 or 48 ports and can be configured by a web or command-line interface. An aggregate switch is used to aggregate data from multiple switches and forward it to a core switch. A power diode switch is used for lights.

10. The correct answer is **D**. A hub is an internal legacy device that was implemented to connect hosts using 10BASE-T Ethernet cabling. All other answers are incorrect. A load balancer receives client requests and sends them to the least utilized host. These servers all perform the same job function. A switch is a more modern device that connects hosts but, unlike the hub, can send the traffic to one particular host and is therefore a faster replacement for the hub. A router is a device that connects networks together.

11. The correct answer is **C**. A firewall and router control access by an access control rule (ACL). When installed, only one rule is set up: the last rule, deny. When traffic arrives at the firewall and there is no allow rule, the last rule of deny will be applied. This is known as implicit deny. All other answers are incorrect. No allow rule means the document will be blocked. The document will be blocked at the network level and therefore will never get as far as the host. Explicit deny occurs when a deny rule has been set up on the firewall.

12. All statements are true.

13. The correct answers are **A**, **C**, and **D**. The application layer applies business logic to prioritize traffic. The control layer contains routing information and is inserted between the application and infrastructure layer and uses a virtual device known as the SDN controller. The infrastructure layer handles the routing and switching of traffic. All other answers are incorrect. The transport layer uses TCP or UDP for the delivery of packets. The data link layer provides error control and framing, moving from the physical layer to the network layer. The physical layer defines the connection and transmission types, such as Ethernet, wireless, or token ring.

14. The correct answer is **B**. Cat 5 cable is a type of Ethernet cable that uses an RJ45 connector. All other answers are incorrect. A BNC connector uses a coax cable. An RJ11 connector is used to connect a modem to a telephone line. A Cat 3 cable runs at 10Mbps while Cat 5 runs at 100Mbps.

15. The correct answer is **B**. 802.3at (POE+) allows powered devices to draw up to about 25W. All other answers are incorrect. 802.11 is a wireless standard. 802.3af allows powered devices to draw up to about 13W. 802.3bt (POE++ or 4PPOE) allows powered devices to draw up to 51W (type 3) or 71W (type 4).

16. The correct answers are **B** and **D**. Asymmetrical Digital Subscriber Line (ADSL) has a faster download than upload speed, and symmetric DSL has the same upload and download speed. All other answers are false.

2.3 Compare and contrast protocols for wireless networking

1. The correct answers are **A**, **C**, **D**, and **E**. Only Wi-Fi 5 is incorrect. Wi-Fi 6 (802.11ax), 802.11 b and g, and Wi-Fi 4 (802.11n) all operate on 2.4GHz. Wi-Fi 5 (802.11ac) operates at 5GHz.

2. The correct answer is **D**. Wi-Fi 6 (802.11ax) operates in both the 2.4GHz and 5GHz ranges, thus creating more available channels. Wi-Fi 6 chipsets support a total of 12 channels, eight in the 5GHz and four in the 2.4GHz range. All other answers are incorrect. 802.11b supports 2.4GHz. 802.11g supports 2.4GHz, and 802.11a supports 5GHz.

3. The correct answer is **D**. The user should go to Settings on the smartphone, enable Bluetooth, then pair the device. All other answers are incorrect.

4. The correct answer is **B**. Long-range fixed wireless can be used as a bridge to connect two wireless networks and can be either licensed or unlicensed. All other answers are incorrect. GPS is used to determine your latitude and longitude using orbital satellites. Unlicensed wireless networks use a public frequency and interference is a risk. Licensed wireless networks are those for which exclusive rights are purchased to a given frequency band within a given geographical area from the relevant regulator.

5. The correct answer is **C**. Near-Field Communication (NFC) is used for short-range contactless payments. All other answers are incorrect. Bluetooth is used to connect devices wirelessly and share data. RFID is used to tag high-value items to prevent them from being stolen. Tethering is the protocol whereby your phone is used to create an internet connection for a laptop or desktop using a data cable.

6. The correct answer is **A**. 802.11a is 5GHz only. All other answers are incorrect. 802.11b and 802.11g are 2.4GHz only. 802.11n uses both 2.4 and 5GHz, known as Multiple Input Multiple Output (MIMO). It can multiplex signal streams from 2-3 separate antennas.

7. The correct answers are **A** and **C**. 2.4GHz is both slower and covers a greater distance than 5GHz. All other answers are incorrect.

8. The correct answer is **B**. 802.11ax goes up to 3.5GBps. All other answers are incorrect. 802.11c goes up to 866 Mbps. 802.11a runs at 54 Mbps. 802.11b runs at 11Mbps.

9. The correct answer is **A**. Both 802.11b and 802.11g work on a frequency of 2.4GHz. All other answers are more modern than 802.11g and are therefore not backward compatible.

10. The correct answers are **B** and **C**. 5GHz is less effective at propagating through solid surfaces, supports more individual channels, and suffers less congestion than 2.4GHz. All other answers are incorrect. 2.4GHz can penetrate solid surfaces much better than 5GHz but supports fewer channels and therefore suffers more congestion.

11. The correct answer is **D**. 802.11n uses both 2.4 and 5GHz, which is known as Multiple Input Multiple Output (MIMO). It can multiplex signal streams from 2-3 separate antennas. All other answers are incorrect. 802.11a is 5GHz only. 802.11b and 802.11g are 2.4GHz only.

2.4 Summarize services provided by networked hosts

1. The correct answer is **C**. The Dynamic Host Configuration Protocol (DHCP) server allocates an IP address to each host, and this should be checked first. All other answers are incorrect. A domain controller authenticates hosts. A DNS server provides name resolution and would be an issue if you could not access websites. A mail server provides users with access to email.

2. The correct answer is **D**. When you have network connectivity but cannot access any websites, it means that you cannot access a DNS server. All other answers are incorrect. If you have an internet connection, then your log-on has been successful. If you have an internet connection, then your IP address is valid. There is no need to check the web server location as it will not change.

3. The correct answer is **B**. A proxy server can do webpage caching. All other answers are incorrect. File servers store documents. UTM firewalls can provide content filtering, URL filtering, and malware inspection. Web servers host websites but cannot cache the pages.

4. The correct answer is **C**. A SCADA network is an industrial control system that can be used in the production of oil or gas. All other answers are incorrect. There is no such network as a production network. A local area network is not used in the production of oil or gas but rather hosts many users and devices. A Metropolitan Area Network (MAN) is a network within a city used by either the police, ambulance, or fire services.

5. The correct answers are **A** and **C**. IoT devices need access to the internet and often fall into the category of home automation. Alexa is used by many households to find out facts or play music. A smart meter can tell you the amount of energy that you use and at the same time update your energy supplier. All other answers are incorrect. Neither alarm clocks nor headsets require internet access.

6. The correct answers are **A**, **C**, and **D**. A spam gateway prevents spam from entering your network using SPF, DKIM, and DMARC. It also uses DLP to prevent PII and other sensitive information from leaving your network and filters incoming messages to users' mailboxes. However, an organization will never send out spam through a spam gateway.

7. The correct answer is **B**. A load balancer can deal with a high volume of web traffic and route it to the least-utilized host. Installing one ensures that all web servers are utilized efficiently. All other answers are incorrect. A cluster is two servers sharing a quorum disk to provide high availability. A proxy server filters outgoing traffic and caches webpages. A DNS server provides hostname-to-IP-address name resolution.

8. The correct answer is **D**. A mail server uses Simple Mail Transfer Protocol (SMTP) to transfer email using port 25. All other answers are incorrect. DNS servers use port 53. DHCP servers use ports 67/68. Proxy servers use port 8080.

9. The correct answer is **B**. A web server hosts websites, each of which has a home page through which customers can access applications and information about a product or service. All other answers are incorrect. A file server is an internal service that hosts data. A mail server contains mailboxes. A RADIUS server, also known as an AAA server, provides authentication from supplicants.

10. The correct answer is **B**. \\server1\data is a UNC path used to connect either to a file or print service. Since the name of the share is data, it will be a file share. All other answers are incorrect. A print server allows someone to send documents to a printer. A syslog server centralized log files from multiple servers. A proxy server caches website pages and controls outbound traffic via URL and content filters.

11. The correct answer is **D**. A RADIUS server is an AAA server that provides authentication, authorization, and accounting without needing to hold a copy of the directory services. Supplicant is another name for devices such as VPN servers, switches, and access points. All other answers are incorrect. A syslog server centralizes log files from multiple sources. A DNS server provides hostname-to-IP-address resolution. A proxy server caches webpages and handles URL and content filtering.

12. The correct answer is **C**. It is likely that the driver for the operating system is not on the installation media. Therefore, we need to download the up-to-date driver from the manufacturer's website. All other answers are incorrect.

13. The correct answer is **A**. A syslog server is also known as a log collector and centralizes log files from multiple servers. All other answers are incorrect. A file server hosts documents that are to be accessed by members of the domain. A domain controller authenticates users within a domain.

14. The correct answer is **D**. IoT devices have default passwords that can be found on search engines. Because the device is connected to the internet, a hacker could use these publicly available passwords and gain access to your home network. Therefore, the first thing the user should do is reset the default password to something more secure. All other answers are incorrect. Some IoT devices have no means of updating and this is not the main priority. If you disconnect an IoT device from the internet, it will not function as it is an internet-connected device. Reading the user manual is important but not as important as your home security.

2.5 Given a scenario, install and configure basic wired/wireless small office/home office (SOHO) networks

1. The correct answer is **B**. A static address is set up manually, and a server or printer IP address should never change. All other answers are incorrect. Dynamic addresses are allocated by DHCP. These addresses could continually change, and users will have difficulty connecting to it. APIPA cannot be set up as they are allocated when a fault has been detected. Servers can be allocated either a public or private IP address, but static is more relevant.

2. The correct answer is **A**. Private IP addresses can only be used in an internal network. All other answers are incorrect. Private IP addresses can be used in networks with up to 16,777,214 hosts. Every IPv4 address has a network ID and a host ID.

3. The correct answer is **A**. 131.107.1.1 is a Class B public IP address. All other answers are incorrect. 192.168.1.1 is a private IP address. 169.254.1.223 is an APIPA that is allocated. You cannot get an IP address from DHCP. 172.16.5.14 and 10.10.15.6 are private IP addresses. IP addresses starting 10, 172 and 192 are private IP addresses and can only be used internally. 169.254.x.x is an APIPA and cannot be used externally. Any other IP address ranges than these are public and can be used on the internet.

4. The correct answer is **B**. Class B addresses use the first two octets for the network ID. Therefore, the subnet mask is 255.255.0.0. All other answers are incorrect. 255.0.0.0 is the default subnet mask for a Class A address. 255.255.255.0 is the default subnet mask for a Class C address. 169.254.1.1 is an APIPA address, and you cannot access valid addresses from DHCP servers. With this address, you cannot communicate with others on the network.

5. The correct answer is **D**. A home network is more likely to have a Wireless Access Point (WAP) as a home router. All other answers are incorrect. Hubs join multiple hosts together but very slowly. A router is an enterprise product that joins networks together and is normally used in enterprise settings. Switches join multiple internal hosts together more quickly than a hub.

6. The correct answer is **C**. 212.15.1.2 is a valid IPv4 address. All other answers are incorrect. 10.1.1.0 cannot be used for a host as it ends in 0, indicating that it is a network address. Any address starting with 255 is a subnet mask and cannot be used for a host. 12.1.1.255 cannot be used as a host as it ends in 255, indicating that it is the broadcast address.

7. The correct answer is **D**. A Windows server that uses both IPv4 and IPv6 addresses is known as dual stack. All other answers are incorrect.

8. The correct answers are **A** and **D**. A desktop may be allocated a 169.254.x.x address either because it is an Automated Private IP Address (APIPA) assigned due to a duplicate IP address or (most commonly) it is unable to get network connectivity to the DHCP server. All other answers are incorrect. A DNS server is used for hostname-to-IP-address resolution. A domain controller is used for authentication.

9. The correct answer is **B**. The default gateway is missing, and this prevents the user from leaving the internal network. A default gateway is required to access the internet. All other answers are incorrect. If the gateway was present, then DNS might be an issue with the same scenario, but this is not the case. 132.24.0.1 is a public Class B address and therefore can get onto the internet. You would need to run ipconfig /all to determine whether the IP address is dynamic or static.

10. The correct answer is **A**. An IPv4 address has 4 octets of 8, making it a 32-bit addressing schema. All other answers are incorrect.

11. The correct answer is **D**. 2001:0dC8:0000:0000:0abc:0000:def0:2311 is an IPv6 address. All other answers are incorrect. 10.1.1.1 is a private IPv4 address. B4-2E-99-C0-75-45 is a MAC address. 169.254.1.5 is an APIPA address used to contact the DHCP server or results from a duplicate IP address being allocated.

12. The correct answer is **C**. If you cannot access the internet, it is most likely to be the router's gateway or a DNS problem. All other answers are incorrect. NETBIOS is a legacy naming convention. Server Message Block (SMB) traffic is a communication protocol that allows access to file shares and printers. SMTP is used to transfer mail between mail servers.

13. The correct answer is **D**. When you shorten an IPv6 address, you remove the leading zeros. Therefore, 0dc8 becomes dc8. Then you look at the third and fourth octets, which are 0000:0000. This can be replaced by ::. You know there are 8 octets, so when you count six remaining, you know 0000:0000 is missing. You then take 0abc and remove the leading zero, leaving abc. The sixth octet is 0000, but you cannot use :: again, so you reduce it to :0:. Thus, the shortened IPv6 address becomes 2001:dC8::abc:0:def0:2311. All other answers are incorrect.

14. The correct answer is **C**. 126.1.1.1 is a public IPv4 address. All other answers are incorrect. The IPv4 addresses 10.10.10.1, 172.16.1.3, and 192.168 are all private. Any addresses starting with 10, 172.16-172.31, or 192.168 are private and cannot be used externally.

15. The correct answer is **D**. An IPv6 address has 64 bits for the network ID and 64 bits for the interface ID, making it a 128-bit addressing schema. All other answers are incorrect. IPv4 uses 32-bit addressing.

2.6 Compare and contrast common network configuration concepts

1. The correct answer is **A**. It is most likely that the financial director has an APIPA, and that is why they cannot connect to anyone else. Check to see whether the DHCP server has allocated an IP address. All other answers are incorrect. Simple Network Management Protocol (SNMP) monitors the status of and creates reports on network devices. RADIUS is an AAA server that controls access to the network, but the administrator is already on the network. A DNS server translates host names to IP addresses.

2. The correct answer is **B**. The address above is an IPv6 address and needs an AAA record. All other answers are incorrect. An A record is used for an IPv4 host. An MX record is used by a mail server. A TXT record is used for any free-form record such as an SPF record.

3. The correct answer is **C**. A Microsoft Dynamic Host Configuration Protocol (DHCP) server has a default lease duration of 8 days. All other answers are incorrect.

4. The correct answer is **A**. An MX record is used for mail servers. All other answers are incorrect. An A record is used for an IPv4 host. An AAA record is used for an IPv6 host. SRV records are used to find services such as domain controllers.

5. The correct answer is **C**. A Local Area Network (LAN) is an internal secure network. All other answers are incorrect. A Wide Area Network (WAN) spans multiple geographical locations. A Metropolitan Area Network (MAN) is used by the police, ambulance, and fire services in a city. CAN refers to a campus area network used in academic institutions.

6. The correct answer is **D**. With DomainKeys Identified Mail (DKIM), an organization uploads a public key as a TXT record. The authenticity of the originating servers of incoming messages can be verified using this key. All other answers are incorrect. SPF uses a TXT record to indicate that a host from a particular domain is allowed to send mail. A syslog centralizes the log files from many servers.

7. The correct answer is **D**. With a DHCP reservation, an IP address is reserved for a host as identified by their MAC address. All other answers are incorrect. A DHCP scope refers to the addresses that a DHCP server can allocate for a particular subnet. IP address lease durations cannot be customized; everyone gets the same lease duration. If a client has a static address that is manually configured, the host will not send out a DHCPDISCOVER packet to try and obtain an address from DHCP.

8. The correct answer is **A**. A Virtual Local Area Network (VLAN) is normally used for departmental isolation or isolation within a LAN. All other answers are incorrect. A proxy server controls access from the internal network to an external network. A firewall is used to control access between the internal and external networks. A router joins multiple external networks together.

9. The correct answer is **C**. DMARC can validate incoming email messages and has the ability to detect and prevent email spoofing. Therefore, any emails arriving from an illegitimate source can be blocked. All other answers are incorrect. A content filter is used by a proxy server or UTM firewall to prevent anyone from accessing a website (such as a gambling site) that has inappropriate content. A proxy server controls outgoing requests and has the ability to cache website content. It can also carry out URL or content filtering by blocking access to websites hosting inappropriate content.

10. The correct answer is **A**. A Dynamic Host Configuration Protocol (DHCP) scope is a range of IP addresses that can be allocated to a subnet. All other answers are incorrect. In a DHCP reservation, the same IP address can be allocated to the same host as identified by their MAC address. A DHCP lease refers to the limited time that a host is allocated an IP address. A DHCP superscope allows two or more scopes to be used as if they were a single scope to increase the number of IP addresses in a subnet.

11. The correct answer is **A**. 131.122.14.12 is an IPv4 address and therefore uses an A record. All other answers are incorrect. An AAA record is used for an IPv6 host. An MX record is used for mail servers. A Sender Policy Framework (SPF) record is used to prove the authenticity of mail servers to prevent spam.

12. The correct answer is **B**. The DHCP handshake sequence is DISCOVER, OFFER, REQUEST, ACK (normally known as DORA). The host sends a DHCPDISCOVER broadcast packet to find a DHCP server. The DHCP server replies with DHCPOFFER containing an IP address along with other configuration, such as the DNS server and the default gateway. The client then replies with DHCPREQUEST to accept the offer. The DHCP server then sends a DHCPACK packet confirming the allocation of the IP address with a lease time of 8 days, normally. All other answers are incorrect.

13. The correct answer is **D**. A Virtual Private Network (VPN) creates a secure tunnel between an external location and the corporate network. All other answers are incorrect. A WAN is an external network (e.g., the internet). SSL is a method of encrypting data in transit, normally via a web browser. DHCP dynamically allocates IP addresses to hosts.

14. The correct answers are **B**, **C**, and **D**. Each company should have one SPF record in the DNS as a TXT file that identifies the hosts that are authorized to send mail. DKIM uses cryptographic keys to verify that the mail server sending the email is authorized to do so. DMARC detects and protects against email spoofing. The remaining answer is incorrect. A stateless firewall is a very basic packet-filtering firewall.

2.7 Compare and contrast internet connection types, network types, and their features

1. The correct answer is **C**. The internet is a Wide Area Network (WAN), due to the large geographical area it covers. All other answers are incorrect. A Metropolitan Area Network (MAN) (such as one used by police) is a network that covers a city. A Personal Area Network (PAN) is used by a single person, for example, Bluetooth. A Local Area Network (LAN) LAN is a network confined to a single location (this could be an entire building or even a single room) connected by one or more switches.

2. The correct answer is **B**. Satellite phones are the only method that are able to communicate in remote areas. All other answers are incorrect. A cable modem would not work as there are no cables to connect to. GPS is used for navigation, and only works via satellite. There would not be any wireless access point up a mountain in a remote location.

3. The correct answer is **A**. Fiber-optic cabling works on light pulses, is immune to EMI, and is very secure. All other answers are incorrect. Coax has many layers that protect against emitting EMI, but, as a hacker could attach a vampire tap and connect to the cable, it is not secure. It is also very slow. Because of the foil layers, STP can reduce EMI but is not as fast as fiber. 10-BASE-T is a legacy Ethernet-cable version and can be UTP or STP. However, it is quite slow (10Mbps).

4. The correct answer is **C**. An iPhone 11 is a smartphone that uses cellular communication (hence the term "cellphone"). All other answers are incorrect. DSL is used to provide internet in a SOHO. An iPhone 11 can use a wireless connection, but this is not the main connection type. An iPhone is not a satellite communication device.

5. The correct answers are B and C. A WISP connects customers and service providers using long-range fixed wireless technology. All other answers are incorrect. A WISP does not manufacture modem wireless access points nor monitor bandwidth.

6. The correct answer is **A**. A Wide Area Network (WAN) is an unsecure network over a large geographical area. All other answers are incorrect. A LAN is a secure fast network with its users all in close proximity, such as a single floor in a building. A DMZ is a boundary network that sits between the LAN and the WAN. As two of these statements are false, "All of the above" is also incorrect.

7. The correct answer is **B**. A Dynamic Host Configuration Protocol (DHCP) server automatically assigns IP addresses on machine startup. It allows an administrator to create a reservation based on the user's MAC address, ensuring that this particular host gets the IP address to be monitored. All other answers are incorrect. SMTP is used for email and not IP addresses. SSL refers to secure data in transit via a web browser. A DNS server is used to perform hostname-to-IP-address name resolution.

8. The correct answer is **C**. A Wireless Local Area Network (WLAN) is used to connect multiple devices wirelessly. All other answers are incorrect. A PAN is one individual network connecting two devices together, such as the Bluetooth connection between a user's earbuds and a smartphone. A WAN is a network over a large geographical area.

9. The correct answer is **A**. A Digital Subscriber Line (DSL) uses telephone lines as a communication channel. All other answers are incorrect. Satellite communication is not reliant on telephones. Neither fiber nor cable modems use telephone lines either.

2.8 Given a scenario, use networking tools

1. The correct answer is **D**. A loopback plug is used to test a network card or switch port. If you get a solid LED, this then tells you that the port or network card can send and receive data. All other answers are incorrect. Pliers would cut through the cable and are better used to firmly grip objects. A cable stripper scores the jacket of a cable and makes it easy to remove. A punch-down tool is used to terminate wires in the back of the patch panel to the IDC.

2. The correct answer is **C**. A cable stripper scores the jacket of a cable and makes it easy to remove. All other answers are incorrect. A crimping tool is used to connect an RJ45 plug to a cable. Pliers would cut through the cable and are better used to firmly grip objects. A loopback plug is used to test network cards and switch ports to confirm whether they can send and receive data.

3. The correct answer is **A**. A punch-down tool is used to push wires into the IDC. All other answers are incorrect. A crimping tool is used to connect an RJ45 plug to a cable. A cable stripper is used to score the jacket so that it can easily be removed. A cable tester can be attached to both ends of a cable to test the permanent link.

4. The correct answer is **D**. A toner probe can trace an RJ45 cable to the patch panel. All other answers are incorrect. A crimping tool is used to connect the RJ45 connector to an Ethernet cable. A punch-down tool is used to fix each conductor into an IDC. An OTDR is used to analyze faults in a fiber cable.

5. The correct answer is **A**. A network tap allows you to divert network traffic to a secondary device for analysis. All other answers are incorrect. A loopback plug is used to test a network card or switch port. A spectrum analyzer analyzes the input signal against a frequency range within a wireless network. A toner probe can trace an RJ45 cable to the patch panel.

6. The correct answer is **C**. A crimping tool is used to seal the RJ45 into either a T568A or B layout. All other answers are incorrect. A punch-down tool is used to terminate wire pairs into the IDC blocks. A cable stripper is used to score the outer jacket from a cable just enough to allow it to be removed to expose the cable. Pliers are used to firmly grip an object.

7. The correct answer is **A**. A Wi-Fi analyzer is a piece of software that can be installed on a laptop. It will detect any other wireless access points in the vicinity and record the signal strength of the different networks using each channel. All other answers are incorrect. A protocol analyzer will collect packets traveling across the network. A bandwidth monitor measures the available bandwidth on a network. RFID detects objects by using tags, commonly used on high-value items in shops.

8. The correct answer is **B**. A cable tester is connected to each end of a cable and tests each wire in turn and a successful connection will show an LED light. All other answers are incorrect. A loopback plug is used to test a network card or switch port. A bandwidth monitor measures the available bandwidth on a network. An OTDR is used to test fiber-optic cables for faults.

Chapter 3: Hardware

3.1 Explain basic cable types and their connectors, features, and purposes

1. The correct answer is **A**. Copper cables are subject to signal attenuation, which refers to the loss of signal strength over distance. Copper cables can be susceptible to electromagnetic interference. This will reduce speed but is not the main limitation. Bandwidth limitation primarily affects the overall capacity of the network but does not directly impact the speed of data transmission. Insulation-related issues are more likely to cause signal quality problems rather than limiting the speed of data transmission.

2. The correct answer is **A**. An Optical Time Domain Reflectometer (OTDR) is a tool used for troubleshooting and testing fiber optic cables. It sends light pulses into the cable and measures the reflections to identify any issues, such as breaks or signal loss. Wire cutters are used for cutting wires and not troubleshooting fiber optic cables. An Ethernet cable tester is used to verify the connectivity and quality of Ethernet cables. A multimeter is used for measuring voltage, current, and resistance in electrical circuits.

3. The correct answer is **A**. ST connectors are typically used with single-mode fiber cables. Their key benefit is low signal loss, not high data rates. Multi-mode fiber is used for high data rates. They use an ST connector that has a bayonet-style design, and they are easy to install. For high-density networks, LC (Lucent Connector) connectors are commonly used. LC connectors are small form factor connectors that offer high-density connectivity while maintaining excellent performance. Coaxial cables are compatible with various connectors and devices, making them versatile for different applications. They can be easily connected to devices such as TVs, modems, routers, antennas, and video cameras.

4. The correct answer is **A**. Cat 5 cables are designed for Ethernet networking and have a maximum distance limitation of 100 meters. All other options are beyond the 100 m limitation.

5. The correct answer is **A**. A punch-down tool is used to connect wires to the demarc securely. A wire stripper removes insulation from wires. A cable tester verifies cable connectivity and quality but is not specifically used for adding lines to the demarc. A crimping tool is used to attach connectors to cables, but not specifically for adding lines to the demarc.

6. The correct answer is **A**. RJ11 connectors are used for telephony applications to connect telephone handsets to wall jacks. RJ11 connectors are not typically used for connecting computers to routers. Printers are usually connected to computers using USB cables, not RJ11 connectors. Connecting a TV to a cable box typically involves HDMI or coaxial cables, not RJ11 connectors.

7. The correct answer is **A**. Cat 5 cables can support a maximum data transmission speed of 100 Mbps. Cat 5e can run at 1 Gbps. Cat 6 runs at 1 Gbps and Cat 8 runs at 40 Gbps.

8. The correct answer is **A**. Thunderbolt cables are commonly used in Apple's macOS systems for high-speed data transfer and device connectivity. Windows is commonly associated with a wireless or Ethernet connection. Linux is associated with Ethernet cables. Android uses micro-USB or USB-C connections.

9. The correct answer is **A**. A crimping tool is commonly used to create an RJ45 cable. It is used to attach the RJ45 connectors to the ends of Ethernet cables, ensuring secure and reliable connections. A wire stripper removes insulation from wires. A punch-down tool is used to connect wires to the demarc. A multimeter is used for measuring voltage, current, and resistance in electrical circuits.

10. The correct answer is **A**. Lightning to USB cables are commonly used for charging iPhones and other Apple devices. Printers usually require specific printer cables or USB cables with different connectors. A crossover cable is used to transfer data between two computers. Display cables, such as HDMI or DisplayPort cables, are typically used for connecting monitors to laptops or other devices.

11. The correct answer is **A**. A crossover cable where we are connecting two similar devices (e.g., a computer to a computer or a switch to a switch). Straight-through cables typically have the same wiring scheme (either T568A or T568B) on both ends, not a combination of both. Coaxial cables typically use BNC (Bayonet Neill–Concelman) or F-type connectors. BNC connectors are commonly used in professional video and networking applications, while F-type connectors are predominantly used in television and consumer audio/video systems. Fiber optic cables use different connectors, such as SC, ST, or FC connectors.

12. The correct answer is **A**. USB offers a speed of 12 Mbps, while USB 2 offers a speed of 480 Mbps. They do not have the same speed: USB (USB 1.1) has a lower speed of 12 Mbps, while USB 2.0 offers a higher speed of 480 Mbps. USB and USB 2 are specific versions of the USB standard with defined speeds.

13. The correct answer is **A**. Plenum-grade cables have fire-resistant properties to meet the stringent safety regulations in air-handling spaces. Plenum-grade cables are not primarily designed for outdoor use. While plenum-grade cables can support high-speed data transfer, it is not their primary use case. While plenum-grade cables can be used for long-distance connections, their main advantage lies in specific environments rather than distance capabilities.

14. The correct answer is **A**. The metallic shielding around STP cables helps prevent EMI from interfering with the transmitted signals. STP cables are not specifically designed for outdoor use. STP cables can support lengths of up to 100 meters (328 feet) for Ethernet applications, making them unsuitable for long distances. You would never use STP cables in a low electromagnetic interference (EMI) environment.

15. The correct answer is **C**. F-type connectors are a type of coaxial connector commonly used for cable television (CATV) and other video or audio applications. Ethernet network connections use an RJ45 cable. Fiber optic networks typically use different types of connectors, such as SC or LC connectors. Wi-Fi devices, such as routers and access points, use integrated antennas or external antenna connectors to establish wireless connections with other devices.

16. The correct answer is **A**. Wire cutters are used to strip the outer sheath of the cable, then we insert the cable into an RJ45 connector and use the crimper to terminate Ethernet cables with RJ45 connectors. All other options are wrong.

17. The correct answer is **B**. LC connectors are known for their small form factor and high density, making them commonly used in data centers and other environments where space is a concern. While SC connectors are widely used in fiber optic networks, they do not provide a higher density compared to LC connectors. ST connectors are older and larger connectors, not known for their high density. FC connectors, similar to ST connectors, are larger and not known for their high density. They are primarily used in specialized applications, such as high-power or industrial settings.

18. The correct answer is **C**. eSATA (External Serial Advanced Technology Attachment) is specifically designed for connecting external storage devices, such as hard drives, to a computer at speeds of 6 Gbps. USB 2.0 (Universal Serial Bus 2.0) has a maximum data transfer speed of 480 Mbps. HDMI (High-Definition Multimedia Interface) is primarily used for connecting audio-visual devices, such as monitors and TVs, and not storage. VGA (Video Graphics Array) is an older interface primarily used for connecting monitors or projectors for video display.

19. The correct answer is **A**. DisplayPort supports simultaneous video and audio transmission over a single cable, making it convenient for connecting monitors with audio capabilities. DisplayPort does not work with a wide range of older display devices. DisplayPort could be more expensive than other interfaces.

3.2 Install the appropriate RAM given a scenario

1. The correct answer is **B**. The primary purpose of virtual RAM is to improve system performance by extending the available memory. It allows the computer to use a portion of the hard drive or SSD as additional RAM when the physical RAM becomes insufficient. Virtual RAM's purpose is not to provide additional storage for files and documents. Virtual RAM serves as an extension of the available memory, rather than a backup solution. Virtual RAM has nothing to do with CPU and GPU.

2. The correct answer is **A**. The primary reason for using DDR RAM in computer systems is its improved data transfer rates. DDR RAM enables data transfer on both the rising and falling edges of the clock signal, effectively doubling the transfer rate compared to earlier memory technologies. This boost in speed enhances system performance and responsiveness. DDR RAM is not used for increasing storage capacity in computer systems. DDR RAM is not used for power efficiency; the main reason is increased data transfer rates. DDR RAM can contribute to reducing latency to some extent; its primary purpose is to enhance data transfer rates.

3. The correct answer is **D**. SODIMM RAM (Small Outline Dual Inline Memory Module) is the type of memory module commonly used in laptops and small form factor computers due to its compact size. DIMM RAM (Dual Inline Memory Module) is a larger form factor memory module typically used in desktop computers. RIMM RAM (Rambus Inline Memory Module) is an older memory module type that was used in high-end workstations or servers that demanded high-speed memory access and data transfer rates. MicroDIMM RAM is a smaller variant of DIMM RAM commonly found in specialized or niche devices.

4. The correct answer is **C**. ECC RAM is designed to detect and correct memory errors, improving data integrity. ECC RAM is not specifically designed to provide faster data transfer between the CPU and RAM. Its main focus is error detection and correction rather than improving transfer speeds. ECC RAM does not enhance graphics processing capabilities. ECC RAM does not increase the storage capacity of RAM.

5. The correct answer is **B**. The primary benefit of using dual-channel RAM is faster data transfer rates. It utilizes two differently colored memory slots, allowing for parallel data access and improving overall system performance. Typically, a black slot and a contrasting color such as blue, gray, or white, depending on the manufacturer. Dual-channel RAM does not directly increase the storage capacity of the RAM. Dual-channel RAM does not directly improve graphics performance. Dual-channel RAM does not specifically lower power consumption.

6. The correct answer is **C**. The primary advantage of using quad-channel RAM is improved data transfer rates. It utilizes four memory channels simultaneously, allowing for increased bandwidth and faster data transfer between the RAM and the CPU. Quad-channel RAM does not have any effect on storage. While quad-channel RAM can offer some benefits for multitasking scenarios, it is not its primary advantage. Memory latency is more influenced by factors such as memory speed and timings.

7. The correct answer is **A**. DDR2 goes from 400 to 1,066 MHz, DDR3 goes from 800 to 2,133 Mhz, and DDR4 goes from 2,133 to 3,200 MHz. All other options are wrong.

8. The correct answer is **D**. The combination of an SSD, Intel Core i7 CPU, and 16 GB DDR4 RAM is the best choice for a gaming PC due to faster storage access, high-performance processing capabilities, and ample memory capacity. SSD, Intel Core i5, 8 GB DDR4, offers a good balance, but a higher-end CPU such as the Intel Core i7 is preferred for gaming. 16 GB of DDR4 RAM provides a more comfortable gaming experience. An SSD is preferred over an HDD for faster loading times, while AMD Ryzen 3 CPUs and DDR3 RAM are less powerful options compared to the others for gaming purposes.

3.3 Given a scenario, select and install storage devices

1. The correct answer is **C**. The primary advantage of installing an M.2 hard drive directly on the motherboard without cables is the simpler and more secure connection. It eliminates the need for extra cables and reduces clutter within the system. Faster data transfer rates are not the main advantage. The IDE is an older interface used for traditional hard drives and optical drives, and it does not apply to M.2 drives. Increased storage capacity is not the primary advantage of installing M.2 drives without cables.

2. The correct answer is **B**. 1 TB NVMe SSDs offer significantly faster data transfer rates compared to traditional hard drives, such as SATA SSDs or HDDs. They provide improved performance, lower latency, and faster access times, making them the optimal choice for maximizing speed. eSATA is not used as a hard drive but it is used for external storage. A USB 3.0 flash drive will not be used as a hard drive but is slower than NVMe SSD. A 1 TB SATA SSD is not as fast as an NVMe SSD.

3. The correct answer is **A**. Slower rotational speeds of 5,400 rpm result in slower data access and transfer rates due to the increased time taken by the read/write head to locate and access data on the spinning disk. 7,200 rpm, 10,000 rpm, and 15,000 rpm are all faster than 5,400 rpm.

4. The correct answer is **A**. Flash drives, commonly known as USB drives are used for portable storage due to their convenience and ease of use. Memory cards are also used for portable data storage. Optical drives are used for reading or writing optical disks. Hard disk drives are used internally in the system.

5. The correct answer is **A**. When selecting a motherboard for a specific CPU, a critical consideration is ensuring socket compatibility. The CPU socket on the motherboard must match the socket type of the CPU for proper physical and electrical connections. Memory type support is important but not critical, but it will tell you how much and what type of memory the motherboard supports. Expansion slot availability is important for adding additional components, but it is not critical. Form factor compatibility ensures that the motherboard fits into the computer case, but it is not the main factor when choosing a motherboard for a specific CPU.

6. The correct answer is **C**. Optical drives, such as CDs or DVDs, are used for reading or writing optical disks. Flash drives use solid-state memory and do not rely on laser technology for reading and writing data. Memory cards, such as SD or microSD cards, also do not use laser technology for data storage. SSDs use flash memory technology for data storage and do not require laser technology for data access.

7. The correct answer is **A**. A SATA cable has a small, L-shaped connector at one end and a flat connector at the other end. A wide, rectangular connector at both ends would be an IDE cable. An audio/video cable would be a round, barrel-shaped connector at one end and a flat connector at the other end. A triangular-shaped connector at one end could be a DisplayPort cable or an HDMI cable.

8. The correct answer is **D**. HDDs with 15,000 rpm are used in specialized enterprise environments requiring high-performance storage due to their faster data access and transfer rates. However, they may generate more heat and noise compared to HDDs with lower rotational speeds, such as 5,400 rpm, 7,200 rpm, or 10,000 rpm.

9. The correct answer is **C**. RAID 5 uses a minimum of three drives, which distributes data and parity across the drives, providing both data redundancy and increased storage capacity. RAID 0 does not provide data redundancy and would not be suitable for ensuring data protection in this case. RAID 1, which mirrors the data across the drives only uses two drives. RAID 10, which combines striping and mirroring, would require a minimum of four drives to implement.

10. The correct answer is **A**. PCIe is commonly used for connecting high-speed graphics cards in computer hardware. It provides a high-bandwidth interface that enables fast communication between the graphics card and the motherboard. This allows for optimal performance and rendering of complex graphics, resulting in enhanced gaming experiences and improved graphics-intensive applications. All other options are incorrect.

11. The correct answers are **A** and **D**. RAID 6 uses a minimum of four drives, which distributes data and parity across the drives, providing both data redundancy and increased storage capacity. RAID 10 also uses a minimum of four drives, which combines striping and mirroring, providing both data redundancy and increased storage capacity. RAID 0 does not provide data redundancy and would not be suitable for ensuring data protection in this case. RAID 5 requires a minimum of three drives.

12. The correct answer is **B**. RAID 1, also known as mirroring, duplicates the data across the two drives, providing redundancy in case one drive fails and the other drive takes over. RAID 0, also known as striping, does not provide data redundancy. RAID 5 needs a minimum of three drives and RAID 10 a minimum of four drives.

13. The correct answer is **B**. Memory cards, such as SD or microSD cards, can be used for data storage. Flash drives can be used in digital cameras and smartphones, but memory cards are a much better option. Optical drives are not used in digital cameras and smartphones. SSDs are used in various devices, including computers and laptops, but are not used as expansion storage in digital cameras and smartphones.

14. The correct answer is **B**. M.2 NVMe SSDs provide the fastest data access speeds for laptops. They utilize the NVMe interface and offer significantly faster performance compared to other SSD options. 2.5" SAS HDDs provide high reliability and integrity and are not the best choice for achieving the fastest data access. IDE HDDs are slow legacy hard drives. mSATA SSDs offer faster data access but are slower than M.2 NVMe SSDs.

15. The correct answer is **A**. The main difference between a 2.5" SSD and a 3.5" SSD is their physical form factor and size. A 2.5" SSD is smaller and commonly used in laptops and small form factor desktops, while a 3.5" SSD is larger and typically intended for use in traditional desktop computers. This size difference affects their compatibility with drive bays and installation methods. Both 2.5" and 3.5" SSDs typically operate with the same power. The data transfer speed of an SSD is not directly related to its physical size. 2.5" and 3.5" SSDs determine their compatibility with different drive bays, but this is not the key difference between them. The form factor primarily affects their physical dimensions and installation options.

3.4 Given a scenario, install and configure motherboards, central processing units (CPUs), and add-on cards

1. The correct answer is **C**. NVMe SSDs require a specific NVMe-compatible motherboard with an M.2 slot. All other options are incorrect.

2. The correct answer is **B**. x86 architecture, also known as 32-bit processors, has a maximum addressable memory limit of 4 GB. 2 GB is incorrect as it underestimates the maximum RAM capacity. x64 architecture, also known as 64-bit processors can address memory higher than 4 GB.

3. The correct answer is **A**. In the BIOS settings, ensure that the desired operating system is set as the first boot option. All other options are incorrect as they are unrelated to boot option troubleshooting.

4. The correct answer is **D**. Heat sinks and fans are essential components in desktop computers to dissipate heat generated by the CPU. As the CPU performs computations, it generates heat, and if not properly managed, it can lead to overheating. Heat sinks are designed to absorb and disperse the heat away from the CPU, while fans provide airflow to carry the heat away from the heat sink. Heat sinks and fans do not focus on power consumption, speed of data transfer, or EMI.

5. The correct answer is **A**. The ITX form factor is commonly chosen when building a compact and portable gaming PC. The small size of ITX motherboards allows for a more compact system build, making it easier to transport and suitable for LAN parties or gaming on the go. Other options are not ideal scenarios for using an ITX form factor. They typically require motherboards with more expansion slots and connectivity options.

6. The correct answer is **A**. The primary advantage of liquid cooling over air cooling is improved thermal efficiency. Liquid cooling systems, such as all-in-one (AIO) coolers or custom loops, are designed to effectively dissipate heat from the components, resulting in lower temperatures compared to air cooling. This enhanced thermal efficiency allows for better overclocking potential and overall improved performance of the system. All other options are incorrect.

7. The correct answer is **C**. Performing a TPM reset clears the previous encryption key stored in the TPM and establishes a fresh secure connection with the upgraded hardware, allowing the system to boot and regain access to the stored data. Disabling the TPM functionality in the BIOS may prevent the system from accessing the encrypted key required to decrypt the data. Reverting to the previous hardware configuration might not be practical or necessary, and it does not address the issue of the TPM encryption key.

8. The correct answer is **A**. A clicking noise during computer bootup may indicate a failing hard drive with mechanical issues such as a malfunctioning read/write head or a failing spindle motor. Promptly backing up the data and replacing the failing hard drive is crucial to prevent data loss. An overheating CPU can cause the computer to shut down. A loose power cable might result in power loss. A malfunctioning graphics card is not related to a clicking noise.

9. The correct answer is **A**. The 8-pin EPS connector is commonly used to provide dedicated power to the CPU on a desktop motherboard. It ensures stable and sufficient power delivery to meet the high power demands of modern CPUs. The 4-pin Molex connector is commonly used for connecting fans and cooling devices. The 6-pin PCIe connector is used to provide supplementary power to PCIe expansion cards, such as graphics cards. The 24-pin ATX connector is the primary power connector for the motherboard.

10. The correct answer is **A**. Operating a disk infrastructure in a degraded state increases the risk of data loss. When one or more disks in the infrastructure are degraded or experiencing issues, the system relies on the remaining disks to maintain data integrity. All other options are wrong.

11. The correct answer is **A**. If the CPU fan fails to function properly, it can result in inadequate cooling of the CPU. As a consequence, the CPU may overheat, which can lead to system instability, unexpected shutdowns, or even permanent damage to the CPU. Proper cooling is essential for maintaining the CPU's optimal temperature and ensuring its reliable operation. The CPU's performance may decrease but it is not the primary reason. All other options are incorrect.

12. The correct answer is **A**. A continuous beep from a computer typically indicates a RAM failure or a compatibility issue. If the CPU is not properly seated in its socket, you may encounter an error such as a "CPU Fan Error" or a "No POST" (Power-On Self-Test) error. Power-related issues will result in experiencing intermittent power loss, sudden shutdowns, or power failure.

13. The correct answer is **A**. The main difference between AT and ATX motherboards is their size and form factor. Other options that are differences but not the main difference are AT is considered legacy where motherboards are larger in size, while ATX motherboards are smaller and more commonly used in modern computer systems. ATX motherboards introduced improvements such as better component placement, standardized I/O ports, and improved power management. AT uses a single power supply whereas ATX uses a 20/24-pin connector. ATX supports more expansion slots compared to AT. ATX supports DDR4 RAM while AT supports the older DDR3 RAM.

14. The correct answer is **D**. When a heat sink is not working optimally, it is recommended to check for dust accumulation and clean the heat sink, as dust can obstruct airflow. Additionally, replacing the thermal paste between the CPU and heat sink helps ensure efficient heat transfer. Finally, ensuring proper contact between the CPU and heat sink is crucial for effective heat dissipation.

15. The correct answer is **A**. The technician should use the BitLocker Drive Encryption tool to unlock and access the encrypted USB drive. By entering the decryption key or password in the BitLocker Drive Encryption settings, the drive can be unlocked, allowing authorized access to the files stored on it while ensuring data security. Disk Clean-up is a tool used to free up disk space by removing unnecessary files. Windows Defender Firewall is responsible for network traffic filtering and protection against unauthorized access. Task Scheduler is used to automate tasks and launch programs at specified times or events.

16. The correct answer is **A**. To prevent unauthorized booting from a CD, implement secure boot. Secure boot ensures that only trusted and digitally signed operating systems can be booted, preventing the use of unauthorized live CDs. All other options are important security measures but they do not directly address the specific scenario of booting from a live Linux CD.

17. The correct answer is **A**. Use a power supply with a higher wattage. If plugging in a device causes the power to the PC to go down, it indicates that the current power supply is not providing enough wattage to support the additional power demands of the device. By upgrading to a power supply with a higher wattage, you can ensure that your PC has sufficient power to handle the device and other components without experiencing power interruptions. All other options are incorrect.

18. The correct answer is **A**. When a CPU runs hot due to worn thermal paste, it can lead to system instability and crashes. High temperatures can cause the CPU to perform slowly and trigger thermal protection mechanisms, resulting in system instability and unexpected shutdowns to prevent damage from excessive heat. Other options are potential concerns associated with high CPU temperatures; they are not directly caused by worn thermal paste.

19. The correct answer is **A**. Increasing the RAM capacity improves the system performance when using multiple applications simultaneously. RAM acts as temporary storage for active applications, enabling efficient management and access to data. More RAM allows applications to operate without frequent data swapping, enhancing system responsiveness. Close unnecessary background processes and applications will not improve performance drastically. Installing a faster SSD (Solid-State Drive) can enhance storage performance and application loading times but may not specifically address multitasking performance. Increasing the CPU clock speed can improve application performance, but it may not be the most efficient solution when dealing with multiple applications simultaneously, as it may lead to increased heat generation and power consumption.

20. The correct answer is **B**. The Molex connector is primarily used for connecting fans and cooling devices. It provides power to the fans and allows for speed control and monitoring. All other options are incorrect.

21. The correct answer is **A**. In a degraded state, one or more disks in the RAID array have failed or are experiencing issues, and the system operates with reduced redundancy and performance until the faulty disks are replaced. None of the other options can work in a degraded state.

22. The correct answer is **D**. When some keys on the keyboard do not work and there is no physical damage, a potential cause could be a misconfiguration in the BIOS settings. Incorrect BIOS settings related to the keyboard can result in non-functional keys. Checking and adjusting the keyboard settings in the BIOS settings can help resolve the issue and restore the functionality of the affected keys. While software compatibility issues, incorrect keyboard layout settings, or outdated keyboard drivers can also cause keyboard problems, in this scenario, the BIOS settings are most likely.

23. The correct answer is **A**. The boot password acts as a security measure, ensuring that only authorized users can make changes to the BIOS configuration and protecting sensitive system settings from unauthorized modification. All other options are incorrect.

24. The correct answer is **A**. HSMs securely store and manage cryptographic keys, providing a high level of security for sensitive information such as encryption keys, certificates, and digital signatures. All other options and incorrect.

25. The correct answer is **A**. The purpose of multithreading in computer systems is to increase parallel processing and improve performance. Multithreading enables the execution of multiple threads or tasks simultaneously, allowing for better utilization of CPU resources and faster completion of tasks. All other options are incorrect.

26. The correct answer is **B**. To enable virtualization in your system, you need to access the BIOS settings and enable the "Virtualization Technology," "Intel VT-x" (for Intel processors), or "AMD-V" (for AMD processors) option. This setting allows the CPU to support virtualization instructions. Updating the BIOS firmware may also be necessary to ensure compatibility and access to the latest features, but is not the main reason. Hardware or installed drivers are not the main reasons virtualization will not run.

27. The correct answer is **A**. Advanced risk computing, such as Intel's Advanced RISC Machines (ARM) architecture and multicore processors, offers improved performance and efficiency compared to traditional computing architectures. The use of advanced instruction sets and parallel processing allows for faster execution of tasks and more efficient resource utilization. All other options are incorrect.

28. The correct answer is **A**. Intel architecture plays a crucial role in enabling high-performance computing applications. With features such as advanced instruction sets, cache hierarchy, and integrated memory controllers, Intel processors provide the performance and capabilities required for demanding computational tasks. All other options are incorrect.

29. The correct answer is **A**. Multicore processors offer increased parallel processing capabilities by integrating multiple CPU cores on a single chip. This allows for the simultaneous execution of multiple threads and tasks, resulting in improved performance and faster task completion times. All other options are incorrect.

30. The correct answer is **B**. Intel Core M processors are specifically designed for ultra-thin notebooks, tablets, and 2-in-1 detachable devices. All other options are incorrect.

3.5 Given a scenario, install or replace the appropriate power supply

1. The correct answer is **A**. Modular power supplies allow you to detach and connect only the necessary cables, minimizing cable mess inside the computer case. This improves airflow and facilitates easier maintenance and upgrades. All other options are incorrect.

2. The correct answer is **A**. Installing dual power supplies with separate power sources ensures an uninterrupted power supply by providing redundant backup in the event of a power failure. Redundant power supplies do not affect storage capacity. Redundant power supplies do not enhance CPU performance. Redundant power supplies do not improve network connectivity.

3. The correct answer is **A**. 3.3V: Orange or yellow (typically used in motherboards, network cards, and certain digital circuits); 5V: Red (commonly used in USB ports, power supplies, and various peripherals); 12V: Yellow or blue (frequently employed in power supplies, SATA connectors, and fans). All other options are wrong.

4. The correct answer is **A**. ATX motherboards commonly use a 20-pin or 24-pin power connector, which supplies power to the motherboard and its components. These motherboards are widely used in desktop computers and provide various expansion slots and features to accommodate different hardware configurations. Mini-ITX (Information Technology eXtended) motherboards are compact and designed for small form factor systems. Micro-ATX motherboards are a smaller form factor variant of ATX motherboards. ITX (Information Technology eXtended) motherboards, including both Mini-ITX and Nano-ITX variants, are designed for ultra-compact systems.

5. The correct answer is **A**. The main benefit of a modular power supply is the ability to customize cable management. With modular power supplies, you can connect only the necessary cables, resulting in a cleaner and more organized system. This improves airflow, enhances aesthetics, and simplifies maintenance and upgrades. High efficiency is not the primary advantage of modular power supplies. Modular power supplies do not impact cooling performance. Modular power supplies do not provide increased power output.

6. The correct answer is **A**. In North America, the standard voltage for electrical devices is in the range of 110-120 VAC (Volts AC). This voltage range is commonly used for residential and commercial applications in North America and are designed to deliver power within this range. On the other hand, in Europe and many other regions around the world, the standard voltage for electrical devices is in the range of 220-240 VAC. All other options are wrong.

7. The correct answer is **A**. Redundant power supplies ensure uninterrupted power flow by utilizing backup power sources or UPS systems during outages, minimizing downtime, and preserving productivity in the office. Redundant power supplies do not increase the number of power outlets. Redundant power supplies have nothing to do with office furniture. Backup generators can provide power during outages. They are not considered redundant power supply systems.

8. The correct answer is **B**. For a typical desktop computer, a power supply with a wattage rating of around 500 W is often sufficient. This should provide enough power to support the CPU, graphics card, storage drives, and other peripherals commonly found in a standard desktop setup. 300 W will not give you enough power. 750 W/1,000 W will pull more power than the standard desktop and be used by a gaming machine.

3.6 Given a scenario, deploy and configure multifunction devices/ printers and settings

1. The correct answer is **B**. The carbon paper is not aligned properly in the printer, causing the first page to print lighter. The alignment of the carbon paper in dot matrix printers is crucial for accurate and consistent printing. If the carbon paper is not aligned properly, it can result in lighter print on the first page while the subsequent pages may still be legible. All other options are incorrect.

2. The correct answer is **D**. The primary corona wire charges the photosensitive drum uniformly during the charging stage. This prepares the drum for the subsequent stages of the printing process. All other options are incorrect.

3. The correct answer is **A**. Laser printers utilize a laser beam or LED light source to create an electrostatic image on a photosensitive drum. They also use toner. Dot matrix printers create images by using a series of pins that strike an inked ribbon, producing dot patterns on the paper. Thermal printers use heat to activate special heat-sensitive paper, resulting in the formation of images or text. Impact printers create images by physically striking an inked ribbon against the paper, typically using a series of pins or hammers.

4. The correct answer is **A**. Configuring the MFD with the IP address of an SMTP server. To use the scan-to-email functionality, the MFD needs to be set up with the IP address of an SMTP (Simple Mail Transfer Protocol) server. This server is responsible for accepting the scanned document as an attachment and delivering it as an email. Authentication may also be required by the SMTP server to ensure secure and authorized access for sending the email. All other options are incorrect.

5. The correct answer is **C**. Print servers enable print sharing among multiple computers, allowing them to connect and send print jobs to a shared printer, improving printing efficiency and simplifying printer management. Devices can download print drivers from the print server. All other options are incorrect.

6. The correct answer is **A**. Implementing user authentication and access control measures ensures that only authorized individuals have permission to use the printer. This can be achieved through various methods, such as requiring user login credentials or using access cards/badges to authenticate users before allowing them to print. All other options are incorrect.

7. The correct answer is **B**. Dot matrix printers create images by using a series of pins that strike an inked ribbon, producing dot patterns on the paper. Laser printers utilize a laser beam or LED light source to create an electrostatic image on a photosensitive drum. Thermal printers use heat to activate special heat-sensitive paper, resulting in the formation of images or text. Impact printers create images by physically striking an inked ribbon against the paper, typically using a series of pins or hammers.

8. The correct answer is **A**. The charging stage involves applying a uniform charge to the photosensitive drum using a corona wire. This prepares the drum for the next step in the printing process. In the exposing stage, a laser beam or LED light source is used to selectively discharge the charged areas on the drum, creating an electrostatic image of the printed content. During the developing stage, toner particles are attracted to the areas of the drum that have been discharged, forming a visible image on the drum's surface. The transferring stage involves transferring the toner image from the drum onto the paper or another media. An electric field is applied to pull the toner from the drum onto the paper, resulting in the image being transferred. In the fusing stage, heat and pressure are applied to melt and bond the toner particles onto the paper, creating a permanent image. This is typically done using a fuser assembly that contains heated rollers. After each printing cycle, the cleaning stage ensures that any residual toner or debris is removed from the drum surface. This is important to maintain print quality and prevent contamination of subsequent printouts.

9. The correct answer is **C**. Thermal printers use heat to activate special heat-sensitive paper, resulting in the formation of images or text. Laser printers utilize a laser beam or LED light source to create an electrostatic image on a photosensitive drum. They also use toner. Dot matrix printers create images by using a series of pins that strike an inked ribbon, producing dot patterns on the paper. Impact printers create images by physically striking an inked ribbon against the paper, typically using a series of pins or hammers.

10. The correct answers are **A** and **B**. Poor print quality can be caused by low ink or toner levels, which can result in faded or streaky prints. Additionally, using low-quality paper can also affect print quality, leading to smudges, bleeding ink, or a lack of sharpness in the prints. It is important to ensure both ink/toner levels and paper quality are adequate for the desired print results. The printer driver needing an update would not directly cause poor print quality. Incorrect printer settings may affect print quality, but they are not the primary cause.

11. The correct answer is **A**. The toner on the paper is fused and melted into the fibers through heat and pressure during the fusing stage. This ensures that the toner becomes permanently bonded to the paper and produces a durable printout. All other options are incorrect.

12. The correct answers are **A** and **B**. The issue could be due to the top paper tray having run out of paper and documents are now being printed on more expensive labels. Additionally, selecting the wrong paper tray from the printer settings or in the print dialog can also cause the documents to be printed on labels instead of paper. The printer driver needing an update would not directly cause the issue of printing on labels instead of paper. Low ink or toner levels would not cause the issue of printing on labels instead of paper.

13. The correct answer is **A**. Enable DHCP reservation. By enabling DHCP reservation, you can assign a specific IP address to the printer based on its MAC address, ensuring it always receives the same IP when connecting to the network. A static IP address does not use DHCP. Restarting the router has nothing to do with DHCP. A USB cable has nothing to do with obtaining an IP address.

14. The correct answer is **A**. Configuring the MFD with the path to a suitably configured file server and shared folder. To utilize the scan-to-folder functionality using SMB, the MFD needs to be set up with the network path to a properly configured file server and shared folder. Each user must also have the necessary write permissions on the shared folder to save the scanned documents. All other options are incorrect.

15. The correct answer is **A**. Uploading the scan as a file to a document storage and sharing account in the cloud. When using the scan-to-cloud feature, the scanned document is uploaded and saved as a file on a cloud-based document storage and sharing account, such as OneDrive or Dropbox. All other options are incorrect.

16. The correct answer is **A**. Enabling printing only when authorized users insert a PIN ensures that users are at the printer and therefore prevents print jobs from being sent to the printer and forgotten about. All other options are incorrect.

3.7 Given a scenario, install and replace the printer consumables

1. The correct answer is **C**. The charging stage in a laser printer is performed by the corona wire. The corona wire is a thin wire located close to the photosensitive drum. It applies a uniform charge to the drum, preparing it for the subsequent stages of the printing process. All other options are incorrect.

2. The correct answer is **A**. The type A USB connector is the most common and recognizable USB connector type. It is typically used for connecting printers and other peripheral devices to a computer. The type B USB connector is less common and often used for connecting devices such as scanners. The type C USB connector is a newer, more versatile connector that is becoming increasingly popular. However, it is not the standard connector used for printers. The micro-USB connector is a smaller version of the type B connector and is commonly used for mobile devices, but not typically used for printers.

3. The correct answer is **B**. The wrong paper orientation is selected in the printer settings; the printed document will come out with the incorrect orientation. The printer driver is responsible for the communication between the computer and the printer, but it does not determine the paper orientation. Low ink or toner levels would not affect the paper orientation. The paper size being incorrect would result in printing on the wrong size paper, not necessarily the wrong paper orientation.

4. The correct answer is **B**. Installing the latest printer driver compatible with Windows 10 is crucial for proper functionality. The printer driver acts as a bridge between the printer hardware and the operating system, allowing the computer to understand and send print commands to the printer. All other options may be important, but they are not the most important reasons to ensure functionality.

5. The correct answer is **B**. The printers are connected to a central print server that handles wireless print jobs. In a network with multiple printers, a central print server is typically used to manage and distribute print jobs wirelessly. This server acts as an intermediary between the devices sending the print jobs and the printers themselves, ensuring efficient and organized printing across multiple devices. Setting up separate Wi-Fi networks for each printer would be impractical and inefficient. While printers may have unique IP addresses, they typically communicate with devices through a central print server or network protocols rather than direct communication. Wireless printing eliminates the need for physical connections such as USB cables.

6. The correct answer is **B**. Stereolithography (SLA) is a 3D printing technology that uses liquid resin materials cured by a laser to build objects layer by layer. SLA printers offer high-resolution, detailed prints, making them a popular choice for applications requiring fine details. Fused Deposition Modeling (FDM) is a 3D printing technology that uses thermoplastic filaments, not liquid resin materials. Selective Laser Sintering (SLS) uses powdered materials, typically plastics or metals, to create 3D objects. It does not involve the use of liquid resin materials. Digital Light Processing (DLP) is another 3D printing technology that uses liquid resin materials cured by a light source, typically a digital projector. DLP operates similarly to SLA but with a different light source.

7. The correct answers are **A**, **B**, **C**, **D**, and **E**. They are all correct. Connect the printer to a computer acting as the print server. This computer will manage the print jobs and allow other computers to connect to the shared printer. Install printer drivers on each computer. This ensures that the computers can communicate with the printer and send print jobs. Enable printer sharing in the printer's properties on the print server computer. This allows other computers on the network to access and use the shared printer. Access the network settings on client computers and select the shared printer. This allows the client computers to connect to the shared printer and send print jobs to it. Test the print-sharing functionality by sending a print job from a client computer. This ensures that the print-sharing setup is working correctly.

8. The correct answer is **B**. Printer Control Language (PCL) is commonly used for printing text-based documents without complex formatting, such as simple word processing documents or basic office documents. PCL provides efficient and reliable printing capabilities for these types of documents. PostScript or printer-specific image enhancement technologies ensure accurate color reproduction and precise image rendering. All other options are incorrect.

9. The correct answers are **A**, **B**, and **E**. Removing all protective tapes and packaging materials is essential to ensure that the print device is ready for use and to prevent any obstructions or damage during operation. Leave the device unboxed and powered off for a few hours to reduce risks of condensation forming within an appliance that has moved from a cold storage/transport environment to a warmer installation environment. Print devices are heavy, so make sure you use safe lifting techniques. It may require two persons to lift it safely.

10. The correct answers are **A** and **C**. Heating the extruder to a specific temperature is a common step in replacing filament in a 3D printer. By heating the extruder, the filament becomes soft and can be manually removed, allowing for easy replacement with a new filament. Pull as much of the old filament out as possible, then push the new filament through.

11. The correct answer is **A**. Fused Deposition Modeling (FDM) is a 3D printing technology that uses filament materials, typically thermoplastics such as ABS or PLA. The filament is melted and extruded through a nozzle to build objects layer by layer. Stereolithography (SLA) uses liquid resin materials, not filament materials, for 3D printing. Selective Laser Sintering (SLS) involves the use of powdered materials, such as plastics or metals, rather than filaments. Digital Light Processing (DLP) also uses liquid resin materials, similar to SLA, but with a different light source for curing. It does not use filament materials.

12. The correct answer is **B**. The printer creates its own Wi-Fi network for devices to connect and print wirelessly. Wi-Fi direct is a technology that allows devices to establish a direct wireless connection with each other, bypassing the need for a traditional Wi-Fi network. In the case of Wi-Fi direct printing, the printer acts as a Wi-Fi access point and creates its own network. Devices can then connect to this network and send print jobs wirelessly to the printer. Wi-Fi direct printing does not require an existing Wi-Fi network for connectivity. Wi-Fi direct printing does not use cables. Wi-Fi direct and Bluetooth are separate wireless technologies, therefore Bluetooth cannot be used.

13. The correct answer is **A**. A printer maintenance kit usually contains a new fuser assembly, which is the main component of the kit. Additionally, it includes a transfer/secondary charge roller and paper transport rollers for each tray, which consist of pickup rollers and a new separation pad. These components are essential for maintaining the proper functioning of the printer. Other items such as toner cartridges, ink cartridges, printheads, and additional paper trays are not typically included in a maintenance kit. All other options are incorrect.

14. The correct answer is **A**. PostScript is a page description language that excels at rendering complex graphics and images. It provides advanced capabilities for accurately representing graphical elements, including vector graphics, gradients, and shading. Printer Control Language (PCL) is commonly used for printing text-based documents without complex formatting, such as simple word processing documents or basic office documents.

Chapter 4: Virtualization and Cloud Computing

4.1 Summarize cloud computing concepts

1. The correct answer is **B**. Infrastructure as a Service (IaaS) is a cloud computing service model in which a Cloud Service Provider (CSP) provides the hardware but nothing else. This is ideal when you want to move desktop computers to the cloud. To do this, you would install the operating system, configure it, and patch it. All other answers are incorrect. Software as a Service (SaaS) is a model in which a vendor creates an application, such as Salesforce, and companies lease the application. Security as a Service (SECaaS) is a model in which companies provide cloud identity management services through an external source. An example of this is Okta, which can provide SAML tokens. Monitoring as a Service (MaaS) is a model in which a cloud service provider monitors your network and servers for you.

2. The correct answer is **A**. With a hybrid cloud, a company has employees working in both on-premises and cloud infrastructures. It is the only cloud model that retains on-premises data centers. All other answers are incorrect. A private cloud is a single-tenant model as it is the only entity hosted in that cloud. It can also be hosted on the company's infrastructure. A community cloud is a type of model in which companies from the same industry share resources. Public cloud models use a multi-tenant infrastructure as the CSP hosts many different companies on the same servers.

3. The correct answer is **C**. Infrastructure as a Service (IaaS) provides companies with hardware, but they need to install operating systems, configure them, and patch them. All other answers are incorrect. Platform as a Service (PaaS) provides developers with the tools to create their own customized software. Software as a Service (SaaS) provides common applications on a subscription basis. Disaster Recovery as a Service (DRaaS) is needed when a massive disaster happens, such as a tornado or tsunami.

4. The correct answer is **B**. Software as a Service (SaaS) provides ready-made software. An example of this is Microsoft 365 (M365), which comes equipped with various applications, including Outlook for email, as well as optional add-in applications such as GoldMine and Salesforce. All other answers are incorrect. Platform as a Service (PaaS) provides developers with the tools to create their own customized software. Infrastructure as a Service (IaaS) provides companies with hardware, but they need to install operating systems, configure them, and patch them. Monitoring as a Service (MaaS) is a type of service in which a cloud service provider monitors your network for you.

5. The correct answer is **D**. A private cloud is single-tenant and ensures you have total control over all assets, including the storage and management of proprietary data. All other answers are incorrect. A hybrid cloud is a mixture of on-premises and cloud storage, meaning that not all data would be migrated to the cloud as desired. A community cloud is utilized by a group of people from the same industry sharing resources to create customized applications. A public cloud is a multi-tenant model on which multiple companies share resources and would thus not allow a single company total control of data.

6. The correct answer is **C**. Metered utilization measures the resources that are being consumed by a customer so that they are only required to pay for what they use. All other answers are incorrect. Unlimited resources for free is not a cost-effective option and is not allowable by any cloud service, including metered utilization. There is no reserve pool of resources in the cloud as a CSP can increase or decrease resources at the drop of a hat. There is no restriction for critical resources; you can purchase as many resources as you require.

7. The correct answer is **C**. In a community cloud model, companies within the same industry (for example, a group of law firms or hospitals) share the cost of creating and sharing resources. Each industry has its own software requirements. A private cloud is a single tenant and does not share resources, thereby allowing greater control over stored data than other cloud models. A public cloud model has a multi-tenant infrastructure in which users do not share the cost of creating resources. In a hybrid cloud, a company will both retain an on-premises environment and store some assets in the cloud.

8. The correct answer is **B**. By using a Virtual Desktop Infrastructure (VDI), separate virtual desktops can be allocated to each consultant. VDI uses a pool of virtual desktops with the same configuration, thereby maintaining a consistent desktop. Since the processing of the data is done on the virtual desktop, it secures and protects it against theft. The consultants would need a very low-spec machine that runs a thin client (that is, one that uses only mouse clicks and keyboard strokes) to access it. The company therefore maintains total control of the data. All other answers are incorrect. Once data is downloaded onto a surface laptop (that is, a foreign machine), the company loses all control of the data. Terminal servers are legacy servers that used to be accessed by thin clients, but this technology is now redundant. IaaS only provides the hardware (for example, virtual desktops), but the company still needs to install the operating system and may not be able to provide a consistent desktop.

9. The correct answer is **C**. With Platform as a Service (PaaS), the Cloud Service Provider (CSP) provides the application so that companies can offer their own bespoke (that is, customized) applications, such as MySQL, PHP, Azure, Oracle Database, and Google App Engine, to name a few. All other answers are incorrect. For Software as a Service (SaaS), the vendor has already created an application, for example, Office 365, Salesforce, or GoldMine. Infrastructure as a Service (IaaS) is a cloud service in which the CSP provides the hardware, such as servers, computers, switches, and firewalls. The customer then installs the software, configures it, and patches it. The private cloud is a single-tenant cloud model and would not meet this company's requirements.

10. The correct answer is **D**. The public cloud model is known as multi-tenant as the CSP hosts many different companies on the same servers. All other answers are incorrect. The private cloud model is known as single-tenant as there is only one entity hosted in that cloud. As it ensures exclusive access to resources and is isolated from everyone else, this tenant has total control of their environment. In a community cloud model, companies from the same industry share resources. The hybrid cloud is where a company has infrastructure on-premises as well as in the cloud.

11. The correct answer is **B**. A private cloud model would be the most appropriate purchase for this law firm as it would allow them to isolate their data entirely from all other entities as the single tenant on their host server. All other answers are incorrect. Public cloud models are multi-tenant, and there is a risk of shared tenancy, meaning that another company hosted on the same server would be able to access their data. A hybrid cloud is a model in which a company has some employees on-premises and some working from the cloud, meaning that not all company data would be migrated to the cloud. On a community cloud, companies in the same industry share both costs and resources. Like the public cloud model, this means that the law firm would not retain full control over all their migrated data.

12. The correct answer is **C**. Shared resources means that the cloud provider has a pool of hardware that can be allocated to any of their customers. All other answers are incorrect. Dynamic resource allocation means that a computer or server can adjust the allocation of resources, such as CPU or RAM, according to business demands. There is no such thing as a backup pool. System sprawl means that the consumption of resources by servers exceeds the available resources in a host's virtual environment.

13. The correct answer is **B**. High availability means that a server experiences very little downtime (the five nines), and in fact, observes 99.999% uptime. All other answers are incorrect. VDI is a pool of virtual desktops. Clustering means that two servers share the same quorum disk, in which one is normally active and the other passive; that is, it is on standby waiting for the active server to fail so that it can take over. Shared resources are a pool of hardware resources in a cloud provider's data center that are allocated to any customer that requests additional resources.

14. The correct answer is **C**. Rapid elasticity would allow the toy company to instantly increase and decrease cloud resources according to demand. All other answers are incorrect. Clustering means that two servers share the same quorum disk, in which one is normally active and the other passive, meaning that it is on standby waiting for the active server to fail so that it can take over. Shared resources mean that a cloud provider has a pool of resources that they can allocate to different companies instantly. They are not reserved for any one person. Metered utilization means the CSP will produce a dashboard for a customer so that they can monitor the cost and consumption of resources, such as storage, CPU cores, and bandwidth.

15. The correct answer is **A**. A company could host a private cloud on its own network, ensuring that cloud data is still available if the internet goes down. All other answers are incorrect. A community cloud allows one or more entities to share the storage cost and resources. It is maintained by a CSP and accessed via the internet. With an SaaS, a company develops an application that is leased by companies and accessed via the internet. A public cloud uses a multi-tenant infrastructure in which access to the public cloud is accessed via the internet. None of these three would permit access to cloud data if there is no internet connection.

16. The correct answer is **B**. Virtual Desktop Infrastructure (VDI) is the provision of desktops. The cloud service that relates to this is Desktop as a Service (DaaS), in which the CSP offers VDI (that is, provides desktops). All other answers are incorrect. Software as a Service (SaaS) is where the vendor has already created an application (for example, Office 365, Salesforce, or GoldMine), which you use in its default format. With Platform as a Service (PaaS), the Cloud Service Provider (CSP) provides an application so that companies can provide their own bespoke (customized) applications, such as MySQL, PHP, Azure, Oracle Database, and Google App Engine, to name a few. Infrastructure as a Service (IaaS) is a type of service in which the CSP provides the hardware, such as servers, computers, switches, and firewalls. The customer then installs the software and configures and patches it.

17. The correct answer is **B**. The private cloud model is known as single-tenant as only one entity is hosted in that cloud. It can also be hosted on the company's infrastructure. All other answers are incorrect. In a hybrid cloud, a company has an on-premises environment as well as in the cloud. A community cloud hosts multiple companies from the same industry that share resources. Public cloud models are known as multi-tenant as the CSP hosts many different companies on the same servers.

18. The correct answer is **A** and **D**. Software as a Service (SaaS) is a type of cloud service in which a company develops an application and leases it on a pay-as-you-go model. Your employees can gain access to the application through a web browser. Office 365 provides a built-in email solution, and Spotify is a music platform. All other answers are incorrect. Azure developer tools are an example of Platform as a Service (PaaS) as these tools give you a developer environment where you can build your own mobile applications. Home Depot is an on-premises shop that sells DIY products.

19. The correct answer is **A**. Virtual Desktop Infrastructure (VDI) enables separate virtual desktops to be allocated to each consultant. VDI uses a pool of virtual desktops with the same configuration, thereby maintaining a consistent desktop. Since data processing is done on the virtual desktop, the data is protected against theft. This makes it secure. The consultants would need a very low-level spec machine that runs a thin client (that is, one that uses only mouse clicks and keyboard strokes) to access it. All other answers are incorrect. SaaS is a cloud service in which a company develops an application that is leased by companies and accessed via the internet. The company does not have full control of the desktops. A Virtual Private Network (VPN) is a solution that will create a tunnel across the internet; it does not provide desktops. Remote Desktop Protocol (RDP) is a Microsoft solution for providing remote connections for an administrator to a Windows desktop or server.

20. The correct answer is **D**. File synchronization is an automated advantage of cloud storage that allows the file to be shared across different devices, such as a smartphone and a tablet. All other answers are incorrect. Multiple users can simultaneously access the content. Resource exhaustion means that a computer is running out of resources such as CPU cores, RAM, or disk space. Dynamic resource allocation means that a host can be allocated resources as they are needed; it has nothing to do with cloud storage. File sharing is not an automated process; access to files is done through a mapped drive.

21. The correct answer is **B**. The virtual desktop is on a virtual host, and if there is no network connection, then the desktop cannot be accessed. All other answers are incorrect. In a VDI environment, nothing is copied to the local desktop. Snapshots are a much faster way to recover a guest's machine. A Citrix connection is very fast as it is a thin client, meaning it uses only mouse clicks and keyboard strokes; this makes it an advantage. Disaster recovery being provided by the cloud provider is also an advantage.

22. The correct answer is **D**. Infrastructure as a Service (IaaS) provides the hardware so that the company can move all 10 servers and 50 desktops to the cloud, though they will still need to install the operating system and configure and patch them. All other answers are incorrect. Platform as a Service (PaaS) provides developers with the tools to create their own customized software and mobile applications. Software as a Service (SaaS) provides ready-made software (for example, M365) or common applications such as GoldMine and Salesforce. Monitoring as a Service (MaaS) allows a cloud provider to continuously monitor your network and applications. None of these last three services would be appropriate for the migration described in the given scenario.

23. The correct answer is **B**. Rapid elasticity enables cloud resources to be instantly increased or decreased according to demand. All other answers are incorrect. Rapid deployment describes rapid elasticity but does not exist as a concept in this exam. A load balancer controls access to an array of web servers to give the client a faster browsing experience. Metered utilization means that the CSP will produce a dashboard for a customer through which they can monitor their consumption of resources such as storage, CPU cores, and bandwidth.

4.2 Summarize aspects of client-side virtualization

1. The correct answer is **A**. A Type 1 hypervisor runs on a bare-metal virtual platform. This means that there is no operating system. Examples of this are Microsoft's Hyper V, VMware's ESX Server, and Citrix's XenServer. All other answers are incorrect. Type 2 hypervisors run on software (Windows 10, for example). There are no Type 3 or 4 hypervisors.

2. The correct answer is **A**. A resource pool can be created with additional RAM and CPU cores, which can be allocated to a database resource pool so that the database servers can utilize them as described in this scenario. All other answers are incorrect. System sprawl means that server consumption exceeds host resources in a virtual environment. Network segmentation only divides your network; it does not manage resources. Metered utilization is used by the cloud to charge for the consumption of additional resources.

3. The correct answer is **D**. A Virtual Machine (VM) escape is a type of attack in which an attacker uses a guest virtual machine to attack either another guest virtual machine, the hypervisor, or the host. All other answers are incorrect. Pivoting is a type of attack in which an attacker gains access to a computer on a physical network and attacks another computer or server. VM sprawl means that an unmanaged virtual machine has been added to your virtual network. A snapshot is a backup of a whole virtual machine that can be rolled back when there is a problem with the virtual machine.

4. The correct answer is **B**. Oracle VirtualBox runs on a type 2 hypervisor, meaning that it must sit on top of an operating system such as Windows 10. All other answers are incorrect. A type 1 hypervisor runs on a bare-metal virtual platform, meaning that there is no operating system. Examples of this include Microsoft's Hyper-V, VMware's ESX Server, and Citrix's XenServer. There are no type 3 or type 5 hypervisors.

5. The correct answer is **B, D**, and **E**. A sandbox is a virtual machine that is used to isolate applications in order to safely test new software, examine applications that might contain malware, and ensure that application patches do not have an adverse effect on software. All other answers are incorrect. A sandbox does not contain sand; it has nothing to do with fires. It tests software but not hardware.

6. The correct answer is **C** and **D**. It is possible to build a virtual machine and install a legacy operating system, followed by the legacy application. You can then install Hyper-V on a Windows 11 desktop and import the virtual machine, enabling the legacy application to run. All other answers are incorrect. The application was built for a Windows operating system and is therefore unlikely to run on a Linux operating system. A sandbox is an isolated virtual machine and could not be used to run the legacy application. A SQL server is a database server and should not have any other applications running on it.

7. The correct answer is **A**. Second Level Address Translation (SLAT) improves the performance of virtual memory when multiple virtual machines (guest machines) are installed. All other answers are incorrect. SLAT is not related to networking or throttling the processor. It definitely does not stop virtual memory from being used.

8. The correct answer is **D**. Cross-platform virtualization means that software applications are tested with multiple operating systems, with their own resource constraints, prior to release. All other answers are incorrect. Installing applications on different versions of hypervisors is not a description of cross-platform virtualization. You cannot network sandboxes as they are isolated virtual machines. If you test applications one at a time, you are using the same operating system, not cross-platform virtualization.

9. The correct answer is **D**. Bridged networking is a method by which a virtual client using a type 2 hypervisor is connected to a host virtual machine's physical network card, allowing it to join the virtual network. Here's a reference you can go through: `https://packt.link/UosZ9`. All other answers are incorrect. A Network Address Translator (NAT) hides the internal network when internal users browse the internet. An attacker would join the LAN that the host resides on, not the host itself. A virtual private network is a network that allows guest virtual machines to have their own isolated network.

10. The correct answer is **B** and **E**. The easiest method to accomplish the professor's goal is to use Virtual Desktop Infrastructure (VDI), whereby each student's virtual machine can set its virtual desktop experience to non-permanent. This way, when the students log off, the image will revert to the original image without saving any changes. Another way to do this is to build virtual machines and create snapshots, which can then be reset between classes. All other answers are incorrect. Using a ghost image could take up to 45 minutes to reimage each desktop, which would not be an effective solution if there is insufficient time between classes. Taking a data backup will not resolve anything in this case. Implementing a system could take as long as using a ghost image.

11. The correct answer is **C**. Virtual machine sprawl is where an unmanaged virtual machine is placed on a virtual network. It poses a security risk as the unmanaged virtual machine may not be patched and an attacker could use it to gain access to your network. All other answers are incorrect. System sprawl occurs when servers overconsume host resources in a virtual environment. A sandbox is an isolated virtual machine used for testing applications and software patches and investigating malware.

12. The correct answer is **C**. Fiber Channel provides a very fast connection to a Storage Area Network (SAN) and is the best choice in this scenario. A SAN uses extremely fast disks that are already configured with built-in redundancy. All other answers are incorrect. RAID 0 is neither fault tolerant nor suitable for a virtual network, though it could be used for a proxy server's cache. A Local Area Network (LAN) is not a storage solution. RAID 5 is redundant, but Hard Disk Drives (HDDs) are too slow.

13. The correct answer is **B**. Isolation means that you separate a virtual machine from the guest or another virtual machine. Here's a reference you can go through: `https://packt.link/ URHYE`. All other answers are incorrect. A DMZ is a physical network that sits between the Local Area Network (LAN) and the Wide Area Network (WAN). Docker is used to separate applications from your infrastructure and is particularly useful for developers creating software. A snapshot is a backup of a virtual machine that will allow you to revert to previous settings.

14. The correct answer is **A** and **C**. The problem described in this scenario is virtual machine sprawl, the process of deploying unmanaged virtual machines onto a network. The consultant will likely recommend a two-step solution. The first would be to deploy virtual machines using a template. This would ensure that a consistent baseline is maintained, and the image is patched. The second step is to use SolarWinds Virtualization Manager to prevent virtual machine sprawl, as it has built-in sprawl management capability. All other answers are incorrect. Installing anti-virus on unmanaged virtual machines would be futile. These unmanaged virtual machines might have more vulnerabilities than just anti-virus. Removing these unmanaged machines is a step forward, but it does not prevent reoccurrence.

15. The correct answer is **C**. Virtual Technology for Directed Inputs/Output (VT-d) allows the virtual machine to access the underlying hardware that resides on the host. All other answers are incorrect. When you are preparing to run a hypervisor, you will see an option to turn on Intel VT-d in your BIOS. Here's a reference you can go through: `https://packt.link/POvT5`. Virtual Technology Extensions (VT-x) are used in x86 platforms to allow the virtual machine to access the hardware. A host machine using more than 4 GB of RAM (such as that described) is 64-bit and needs VT-d. Multi-cores allow better performance from the processors. Intel Graphics Virtual Technology (Intel GVT) provides near-native graphic performance on a virtual machine. Neither of these will resolve the current issue.

16. The correct answer is **B** and **C**. An Uninterruptible Power Supply (UPS) is similar to a battery in that it holds a charge and, in the event of a very short power outage, can supply power to the company's servers. If power loss exceeds a few seconds, a UPS can be used to shut down the virtual host gracefully. All other answers are incorrect. The UPS cannot keep the host running if there is a total power loss; that would require a generator. The UPS is a backup power supply and cannot be used to boot up computers, servers, or other devices.

17. The correct answer is **C**. One example of container virtualization is Docker. It only virtualizes the application layer and sits on top of the operating system. This makes writing applications and testing code much more efficient. All other answers are incorrect. A virtual machine backup is called a snapshot. A sandbox is used to test malware. A virtual machine escape occurs when the hypervisor, host, or guest virtual machines are attacked.

18. The correct answer is **D**. Application virtualization is a process by which you can run an application from a remote server, but it has the appearance of running locally. This is great when a virtual machine does not have enough resources to run the application locally. All other answers are incorrect. A sandbox is not a live environment. It is an isolated virtual machine that tests applications and software patches and investigates malware. Installing an application locally on the virtual machine is not how one performs application virtualization. A container such as Docker is used for application development and is not part of application virtualization.

Chapter 5: Hardware and Network Troubleshooting

5.1 Given a scenario, apply the best-practice methodology to resolve the problem

1. The correct answer is **C**. The first stage is to identify the problem with the printer and ignore any solution that a user gives you. After this, you will establish a possible cause, and then test the theory and implement a plan of action.

2. The correct answer is **C**. The junior administrator has violated company policies. The standard operating procedure would state that any server updates should be done out of hours. They did not carry out patch management as that would be an enterprise solution. They just applied a single update to a single server. They did not communicate with users, which is a poor practice but not the main reason for the incident. Since there was no incident before they patched the server, it is not the troubleshooting process we need to look at; therefore, we can rule it out and establish a plan of action.

3. The correct answers are **B** and **C**. The first task that the support technician has is to identify the problem. They will ask the user what they did before the problem occurred and ask whether they made any changes to their laptop, for example, an operating system update. After identifying the problem, they should then back up the data before making any changes. Searching the vendor's website is part of "establishing a plan of action," which comes later in this process.

4. The correct answer is **C**. After the incident has been resolved, the system administrator should document the findings, actions, and outcome. All other options occur before the incident has been resolved.

5. The correct answer is **A**. They have just established a theory of a possible cause. They think that the cause is a recent Windows update. The next stage would be to test the theory, followed by establishing a plan of action. The problem was identified as soon as they started investigating the problem.

5.2 – Given a scenario, troubleshoot problems related to motherboards, RAM, CPU, and power

1. The correct answers are **B** and **D**. When replacing RAM, you should always power down the server and wear an electromagnetic static wrist strap. This will prevent you from damaging the RAM. Putting a machine in standby mode or trying to hot-swap RAM is not a good idea, as either could damage the RAM.

2. The correct answer is **B**. Continuous beeps means that the problem is with the RAM modules or the memory controller. A motherboard problem can be either no beeps or 1 long followed by 2 short beeps. A power supply problem would have no beeps. A video adapter error can be 1 long beep followed by either 2, 3, or 4 short beeps.

3. The correct answer is **B**. Before upgrading the CPU on a server, you should consult the manufacturer's website to identify the socket type of the motherboard. Then, search to see whether that socket type can be upgraded to a faster CPU. Backing up the data, turning the power off, and wearing an electromagnetic static wrist strap should be done prior to the upgrade.

4. The correct answers are **A** and **D**. After installing memory modules, if they are not detected, check the BIOS. If they are not seen in the BIOS, the computer cannot read them; therefore, reset the memory modules to see whether they can be detected. Rebooting the computer will not help and an electromagnetic static wrist strap should be worn but does not detect RAM.

5. The correct answers are **A** and **D**. If maintenance was carried out, the storage adapter cable may have been plugged in with the wrong orientation. Although the technician can hear the fan spinning, the PSU might have a fault preventing the power good signal from being sent to the CPU. Both of these faults will prevent the computer from carrying out the Power-On Self-Test (POST). A motherboard problem can be either no beeps or 1 long followed by 2 short beeps. It is very unlikely that a computer technician will not attach a monitor when booting up a computer.

6. The correct answer is **C**. The clock time on a computer uses the real-time clock that is part of the chipset to keep the time, date, and calendar accurate. The real-time clock is powered by the CMOS battery, and if the clock keeps losing time, then the battery needs to be replaced. The power from the cable to the computer does not affect the computer clock. The PSU does not power the real-time clock. Obtaining a BIOS update does not affect the real-time clock.

7. The correct answer is **B**. A capacitor absorbs spikes in the direct current voltage and then can temporally store charge. If the capacitor is faulty, then it becomes swollen, and if it is not removed, it will blow and cause damage to the computer. The CMOS battery powers the real-time clock and not the capacitor. The capacitor does not store data; the hard drive stores data.

8. The correct answer is **B**. Windows 10 stores keys and biometric data in the local TPM; therefore, if fingerprints are not recognized, we need to clear the TPM. Restoring a system image will not repair biometric errors. Updating the BIOS will not prevent a biometric fingerprint problem.

9. The correct answer is **D**. The problem is a video adapter error. This can be 1 long beep, followed by either 2, 3, or 4 short beeps. A motherboard problem can be either no beeps or 1 long followed by 2 short beeps. It cannot be a normal post because there is an error; however, a normal post would be 1 short beep. A power supply problem would have no beeps.

10. The correct answers are **A**, **C**, and **D**. The first thing to check is that there is power to the wall socket. Then, replace the power cable with a known good cable. After that, plug a lamp into the power socket to ensure you get power. Changing memory will not help power issues. If there was a problem with the memory modules, a continuous beep would be heard.

11. The correct answers are **A** and **C**. This is known as the "blue screen of death" and can be caused by a serious fault – either a system memory fault, a corruption of the operating system, or a device driver fault. A motherboard problem can be either no beeps or 1 long followed by 2 short beeps. Continuous beeps mean that the problem is with the RAM modules or the memory controller.

12. The correct answers are **A, B, C,** and **D.** A burning smell might occur if the CPU fan has stopped working. This will cause the CPU to overheat and the system might reboot or crash. If the heatsink that cools the CPU is not fitted properly or the thermal paste is old, then this can also cause the CPU to overheat. If the PSU is overheating, you will smell burning. If the fan vents are clogged with dust, it will stop the fan from working and cause components to overheat and you will then smell burning.

13. The correct answer is **B.** A computer will perform sluggishly if there has been an incorrect configuration change. A keyboard or a mouse not plugged in will not affect a computer's performance. A computer without a CPU will not boot up.

14. The correct answers are **B** and **C.** On an inkjet printer, a grinding noise indicates that there is a fault in the carriage mechanism. On a hard drive, any grinding or clicking indicates a mechanical problem. A healthy hard drive makes a low-level noise. A motherboard problem can be either no beeps or 1 long followed by 2 short beeps. Continuous beeps mean that the problem is with the RAM modules or the memory controller.

15. The correct answer is **C.** The keyboard has dust or debris stuck under some of the keyboard keys. You should use compressed air to clean between the keys. You should never vacuum a keyboard as it could suck up any loose keys. If you use a wet cloth, you may damage the electronics underneath the keyboard. Equally, sticky keys are an accessibility feature to help disabled people use the keyboard.

5.3 – Given a scenario, troubleshoot and diagnose problems with storage drives and RAID arrays

1. The correct answer is **C.** Redundant Array of Independent Disks (RAID) 5 uses a minimum of three disks and produces a fast read speed. With RAID 5, you can lose one disk and still retain your data. RAID 0 does not provide fault tolerance or redundancy. RAID 1 is called mirroring. It uses only 2 disks, but it does not have the fast read speed that RAID 5 has; it is redundant, and you can lose one disk. RAID 6 uses a minimum of four disks. It provides fault tolerance and redundancy, as you can lose 2 disks.

2. The correct answer is **D.** RAID 5 can function if only one drive fails. If you remove a healthy disk, then the RAID controller will detect a two-drive failure and you will lose all your data. Although the hardware RAID will show the failed disk in red, option C does not answer the question posed. There is a risk with RAID 5 of you removing a second disk from the array, resulting in data loss. Pulling a healthy disk out when searching for the SCSI ID will result in data loss.

3. The correct answer is **C.** SMART is a Self-Monitoring, Analysis, and Reporting Technology tool that monitors the health of hard drives. When an error states that an imminent failure has been detected, then the disk is beyond repair, and you need to replace the disk. All other options are not viable.

4. The correct answer is **C**. If you cannot boot from a hard drive but can see the data by using recovery software, then you should back up the data. At any time, this disk could fail. Although recovery software can access the data, it does not mean that the disk is bootable; therefore, you cannot boot from it even if you install recovery software on it. Formatting the disk will remove the data, and if the disk is not very healthy, it will not function properly.

5. The correct answer is **D**. They will turn on BitLocker on the USB drive and then unlock the disk. The USB drive can now be used. An encrypted USB drive cannot be viewed in Disk Management. Turning BitLocker on in the C drive will not make encrypted data on a USB readable. Converting the USB drive into NTFS will lose all data residing on the USB drive.

6. The correct answer is **C**. The SMART monitoring is reporting errors that are not there; therefore, it is malfunctioning. Disk management is functioning as we can use it to see that all disks are in a healthy state. The filesystem for corporate computers should be NTFS as it provides security. If a disk was missing from the RAID 5 set, then disk management would indicate it was either missing or in a degraded state.

7. The correct answer is **B**. When a computer has a solid orange light, it indicates there is a hardware or driver problem with the hard drive. If there is a problem with the computer memory, you will hear continuous beeps. If the processor has a problem, then the computer screen will be black. If SMART monitoring has been disabled, then there will be no warning when there is a hard drive error.

8. The correct answer is **C**. The first thing we should do is run the system diagnostic program that was supplied with the computer. This should reveal the cause of the extended read/write times. Launching SMART monitoring is a good idea after the system diagnostic check so that you can be notified of imminent disk failure. Swapping out the disk is premature as the system diagnostic test may find that there is a minor error. Disabling SMART monitoring is never a good idea.

9. The correct answers are **B** and **D**. When a disk is in a degraded state, that means that the disk has failed. In a RAID 5 set, one disk can fail and the data will still be available. You should immediately back up the data. You cannot format a disk in a degraded state as it has failed.

10. The correct answer is **C**. When the disk that holds the operating system fails it will generate a "missing operating system" error. If there is a disk missing from a RAID set, the error will say that one of the disks is degraded. If the computer is undergoing a Windows update, it will boot and then notify you it is updating. If the CMOS battery is failing, then the date and time will be wrong.

11. The correct answer is **B**. If you believe that your storage device's performance is degraded, check the input/output operations per second (IOPS) against the manufacturer's baseline. A solid orange light indicates that there is a hard drive failure. Disk management cannot measure the performance of a storage device. A flashing green light indicates that your hard drive is healthy.

5.4 – Given a scenario, troubleshoot video, projector, and display issues

1. The correct answer is **D**. The bulb on a projector has a finite lifespan, and when is it nearing the end of its life, the bulb starts to dim. This is called a burned-out bulb. You might hear a popping sound when it fails completely. Inverters, digitizers, or display settings cannot help a burned-out bulb.

2. The correct answer is **A**. If the projector is displaying a "no signal" error, either the cable is not connected properly or it is faulty and needs replacing. At this stage, the computer is not using its bulb. If the computer's monitor is broken, it should still project the computer's desktop. At this stage, it is too early to extend the display setting as we are not getting any signal.

3. The correct answer is **C**. If the projector has a fuzzy image, then the lens needs to be rotated until the lens shows a clear picture. If the cable was defective, it would say "no signal." The laptop display has no control over a fuzzy image. If the projector bulb needed to be replaced, then the image would be very dim.

4. The correct answer is **B**. The High-bandwidth Digital Content Protection (HDCP) allows a content source (such as a DVD/Blu-ray disc) to disable itself if the display adapter and monitor and/or speaker system do not support HDCP and fail to authenticate themselves with the playback source. If the HDMI cable was faulty, then a "no signal" error would appear. The display setting does not need to be adjusted as there is output on the projector. If there was a problem with the DVD player, then there would be no sound.

5. The correct answers are **C** and **D**. If we get a "no source found" error after changing the cables to known good cables, we need to project from the laptop to the projector. If we run the displayswitch.exe command, then we have four options to project and we should choose duplicate or extend, then the laptop image will be on the computer screen. We can also complete this from the display settings on the laptop. Choose multiple displays and then choose "duplicate these displays" or "extend these displays." There is no need to replace the projector bulb as errors are being displayed. Since the cables have just been replaced, there is no need to check the HDMI cable connection.

6. The correct answers are **A** and **C**. When using a projector from a laptop, if the connectors are not connected securely at both ends, then the screen will flicker. Flickering, flashing images or bright spots around the edges indicate that the backlight is failing. Checking the display setting or rebooting the laptop will not solve anything as it is a hardware error that is causing the problem.

7. The correct answer is **C**. The HDMI-ARC allows the audio from the TV to be sent to an external sound system. If we don't use this port, then the soundbar will not receive any audio from the TV. It is unlikely that the soundbar does not have any power. A soundbar does not have volume control; the volume is controlled by the TV remote. Video resolution has nothing to do with sound.

8. The correct answer is **C**. When a monitor shows either pink or purple discoloration, it is probably caused by a faulty or loose cable. Display burn-in shows a ghost image of the previous image on the screen. The color here covers the whole screen. A faulty graphics card will show a flickering screen but, in this instance, there is no flickering screen. A burned-out bulb will cause the screen to be dim.

9. The correct answer is **B**. When the cursor keeps drifting, then you need to calibrate the screen to fix it. A discolored screen would be a video cable problem. There is no mention of a graphics driver update; therefore, rolling back the driver is not an option. Changing the screen resolution will not fix this problem; it will merely change the size of the screen.

10. The correct answers are **B** and **C**. The projector is overheating, which is why it is intermittently rebooting. We would first check that the fans are working, that no dust or obstruction is stopping the fan from working, and that the air vents are free from dust or obstruction. You might check that the power cable is plugged in properly, but you should not change the cable at this time. The projector display resolution is not the cause of a reboot.

11. The correct answer is **A**. Display burn-in is where the previous image remains on the screen or is shown as a ghost image. Dead pixels are where the screen may freeze, and black areas might be visible. A faulty cable would flicker. The laptop freezing could end up with a "no-signal" error.

12. The correct answer is **C**. Testing the output resolution is primarily done to ensure that the system's output is compatible with a variety of display devices. Display devices can have different resolutions and capabilities, and testing helps confirm that the system can adapt to and function properly with these devices. It ensures that the output is correctly scaled, aligned, and compatible, avoiding issues such as distorted images or cut-off content. The accuracy of color representation and optimization of image quality are secondary considerations, but the main focus is on compatibility with various display devices. It does not enhance system performance.

13. The correct answer is **C**. The display settings is the correct answer as the display settings often include options for touch-screen calibration and enabling touch input. The battery status is incorrect as the battery status does not have a direct impact on touch-screen functionality. The network connection is incorrect as the network connection does not affect touch-screen functionality. The keyboard settings is incorrect as keyboard settings do not directly relate to touch-screen functionality.

5.5 – Given a scenario, troubleshoot common issues with mobile devices

1. The correct answer is **B**. The CMOS battery is the correct answer as a faulty or depleted CMOS battery can cause issues with the computer's ability to retain BIOS settings, leading to POST errors. RAM modules will emit continuous beeping noises. Issues with the hard drive will typically result in boot errors or an inability to access data, but not directly affect the POST process. Graphics card issues may cause display-related problems, but they do not directly impact the POST process.

2. The correct answer is **C**. A PoE injector can supply power to the network device through the Ethernet cable, resolving the power-related problem. Checking cable connections can help resolve physical connectivity issues but will not provide power to the network device. Resetting network settings would not provide power to the device and may not address the power-related issue. Restarting a network device will not resolve the power issue.

3. The correct answer is **C**. The phone's battery is defective when the phone is getting excessively hot. Running resource-intensive apps may cause some heat, but excessive heat is more likely due to a defective battery. Exposure to direct sunlight can cause some heat, but it is unlikely to result in excessive heating. An outdated operating system can cause performance issues, but it is not directly related to excessive heat.

4. The correct answer is **D**. If your phone has liquid damage, you need a professional repair service to repair the phone. Turning on the phone when it has been exposed to liquid can potentially cause short circuits and further damage. Although using rice to absorb moisture is a common suggestion, it is not an effective solution for fully drying the internal components of a phone. Using a hairdryer can introduce heat, which may further damage the phone's internal components.

5.6 – Given a scenario, troubleshoot and resolve printer issues

1. The correct answer is **A**. Duplex printing automatically prints on both sides of the paper. The printing speed of a printer does not necessarily affect paper usage. The type of paper used (recycled or not) does not directly impact the paper usage of a printer. A larger paper tray may reduce the frequency of paper refills but does not address the issue of excessive paper usage itself.

2. The correct answer is **C**. The printer's fuser unit is not functioning properly as it fused the text to the paper. Low-quality ink cartridges may affect the print quality, but they are unlikely to cause the printed text to not stick to the paper. Using incompatible paper might affect the print quality but will not be the cause of this problem. The printer's temperature settings are not adjustable but are based on the specific printing requirements.

3. The correct answer is **B**. The printer's duplex unit is not properly set up. You need to read the manufacturer's leaflet that comes with instructions on how to set it up. Firmware updates are unlikely to resolve a hardware-specific issue related to the duplex unit. The alignment of the paper tray does not directly affect the functioning of the duplex unit. Low ink levels will not affect the printer's ability to perform double-sided printing.

4. The correct answers are **B** and **C**. The printer's drum unit is damaged, or it has dirty feed rollers. Firmware updates generally do not directly relate to the print quality. Low ink levels may affect the print quality, but not marks on the paper.

5. The correct answer is **B**. The paper is too thick for the printer because printers have specific paper weight and thickness limitations, which is why it is failing to feed into the printer. If the paper tray was empty, the printer would not attempt to feed any paper in the first place. Low ink cartridges do not directly affect paper feeding in a printer. Outdated printer drivers can cause various issues, such as printing errors, but not issues with the paper feed.

6. The correct answer is **C**. The most likely cause of a paper jam is any foreign objects or obstructions present in the paper path, such as small pieces of torn paper or debris. These can cause the paper to jam when it is fed through the printer. While an empty paper tray can prevent the printer from feeding paper, it will not cause a jam. While wrinkled or folded paper can cause paper-feed issues, this is not the most likely cause of a paper jam. Low ink cartridges do not directly cause paper jams.

7. The correct answer is **C**. Implementing a login requirement for print jobs allows better control over print resources. Users must authenticate themselves before their print jobs are processed, reducing the likelihood of abandoned or unnecessary printouts, and thus minimizing paper waste. Loading a large stack of paper may lead to increased paper usage and the potential for unnecessary prints, depending on user behavior. While printing double-sided documents can help reduce paper waste, it does not specifically address the need for print job control. Manually feeding paper instead of utilizing paper trays may not be practical for larger print jobs, and it does not directly address the issue of print job control.

8. The correct answer is **C**. The failure of air conditioning can lead to blank spots or missing text on thermal paper due to the print head overheating or improper contact with the paper. To resolve this issue, it is important to clean the print head to remove any dust or debris and ensure that the print head has proper contact with the paper for consistent printing. Overheating and damage to the print head do not address the specific issue of blank spots or missing text. The failure of air conditioning does not directly cause a decreased print speed or slower output in a thermal printer. Thermal printers do not use ink cartridges.

9. The correct answer is **A**. A dirty air filter restricts airflow, causing the projector to overheat. To prevent damage, projectors power down automatically when overheating occurs. An insufficient power supply doesn't directly cause unexpected power downs during operation. A malfunctioning lamp can cause issues, but it's not the most likely cause of unexpected power-downs. A loose connection can cause problems, but it doesn't directly lead to unexpected power downs during operation.

10. The correct answer is **B**. Blank receipts may be printed due to paper feed issues or incorrect paper loading in the printer. Empty ink or toner cartridges can cause other printing issues, but they are not the most likely cause of blank receipts. Overheating of the print head is not directly associated with printing blank receipts. Outdated printer driver software can cause various issues, but it is not the most likely cause of blank receipts.

11. The correct answer is **D**. The ribbon in a dot matrix printer contains ink-soaked fabric or polymer material that strikes against the paper, forming characters or images through impact printing. Inkjet printers use liquid ink cartridges or tanks, not ribbons, to produce printed output. Laser printers use toner cartridges that contain powdered ink, not ribbons. Thermal printers use heat-sensitive paper and do not require ribbons.

12. The correct answer is **A**. When the ribbon becomes worn, it may not transfer ink properly to certain areas of the paper, leading to gaps and missing words in the output. Paper feed issues or misalignment results in skewed prints or paper jams rather than missing words. Overheating will generally affect the overall print quality or lead to other issues, but not specifically missing words. Outdated printer driver software can cause various printing issues, but it is not the most likely cause of missing words.

13. The correct answer is **A**. Excessive heat can damage the print head and lead to poor print quality. Cold print heads will not allow the ink to flow. Maintaining an optimal temperature is crucial to prevent both overheating and clogging problems. Increased temperature can slow down printing. Excessive heat can increase the risk of printer malfunctions but is not the most important factor.

14. The correct answer is **B**. Incorrect label alignment or positioning can cause gaps on printed labels. Gaps on printed labels are typically not related to low ink or toner levels. A paper jam will cause gaps on labels and outdated printer drivers or firmware can cause various printing problems, but gaps on labels are typically related to alignment or positioning.

15. The correct answer is **C**. If the drum is not properly cleaned or has physical damage, it can retain remnants of the previous image, causing a faint duplicate to appear on subsequent printouts. An insufficient fuser temperature typically causes issues such as toner smearing or incomplete bonding, but it does not directly relate to the appearance of a ghost image on the printed page. Low toner levels may result in faded or light printouts. A loose connection between the printer and the computer may lead to communication issues or prevent print jobs from being processed.

16. The correct answer is **D**. If the paper gets stuck to the fuser in a newly installed printer, it is best to contact the printer manufacturer or a technician for assistance. They can provide guidance specific to your printer model and help resolve the issue without causing further damage. Using tweezers or pliers could potentially damage the fuser or other printer components, so it is not recommended. If the paper gets stuck to the fuser in a newly installed printer, turn off the printer and allow it to cool down. Instead of removing the paper yourself, consult the printer's manual or contact the manufacturer for specific instructions. It can provide guidance or recommend contacting a technician to avoid potential damage. Ignoring the problem and continuing to print can lead to additional paper jams or even damage to the printer.

17. The correct answer is **D**. Using an incompatible (third-party) toner can lead to poor print quality and specifically cause lines to appear on copied pages. A clogged printer head can result in inconsistent or distorted prints on both copied and directly printed pages. An overheated fuser would generally affect both copied and directly printed pages, rather than only causing lines on copied pages. Damaged scanning glass would typically result in inconsistent or distorted images on both copied and directly printed pages.

18. The correct answer is **B**. Updating the printer drivers or firmware to the latest version can help resolve the issue. Low ink or toner levels will typically result in faded prints or incomplete text, rather than garbled text. Damaged printer cables or connections could potentially cause printing problems, but not garbled text. Incorrect printer settings or font compatibility can cause printing issues, but they are more likely due to outdated printer drivers or firmware.

19. The correct answer is **B**. Flatbed scanners are commonly used for digitizing a large number of printed documents efficiently and accurately. NFC devices are primarily used for card payments. While a digital camera can capture images, it is not the most suitable or efficient method for capturing electronic images of a large collection of historical handwritten documents. QR scanners are specifically designed for scanning QR codes.

20. The correct answer is **D**. Dust or debris on the imaging drum can cause a consistent line from top to bottom on every sheet. Cleaning the imaging drum using appropriate cleaning methods can often resolve the issue. Low ink or toner levels typically result in faded prints or incomplete text, rather than a consistent line from top to bottom. While a malfunctioning paper feed mechanism can cause various printing problems, it wouldn't cause a single line to be consistently printed from top to bottom on every sheet. A consistent line from top to bottom is not a common symptom of outdated drivers or firmware.

21. The correct answer is **B**. A grinding noise during printing is commonly associated with a paper jam or obstruction. Low ink or toner levels typically do not result in a grinding noise. A grinding noise is not typically related to driver or firmware issues. Network connectivity issues do not typically result in a grinding noise.

5.7 – Given a scenario, troubleshoot problems with wired and wireless networks

1. The correct answer is **A**. Interference can disrupt the wireless signal and limit your ability to choose an optimal channel. Outdated firmware will not limit your ability to choose an optimal channel. Incorrect network configuration settings do not directly affect the ability to choose a specific channel for the router. Insufficient signal strength may lead to connectivity problems, but it does not directly affect the ability to choose a specific channel for the router.

2. The correct answer is **A**. Incorrectly entering a MAC address in the filter list can result in devices that should be blocked being able to connect to the network. Outdated firmware on the wireless router is not related to MAC filtering. Interference from neighboring wireless networks does not affect MAC filtering. Incompatible wireless encryption protocols are not directly related to the MAC filtering functionality.

3. The correct answer is **A**. The client should release its current IP address and request a new one from the network's DHCP server. It is unlikely that the network card has a driver problem. Changing the wireless channel on the router will not resolve the issue. Flushing the DNS cache will not resolve the issue.

4. The correct answer is **A**. The licensed band is exclusively allocated to authorized users with specific licenses, ensuring controlled and interference-free operation. The licensed band requires authorization and is not available for unrestricted public use. The licensed band is not designated for temporary or experimental use; it is reserved for authorized users. The licensed band requires specific licenses; therefore, any unlicensed option is incorrect.

5. The correct answer is **B**. Configure each router on different non-overlapping channels, each with its own IP address range, minimizing interference and optimizing performance. Channel bonding increases bandwidth but will increase interference and worsen latency issues. Since we want a wireless network, we will not be using cable connections. QoS can help manage network traffic, but it may not directly address latency issues.

6. The correct answer is **A**. A VPN establishes a secure and encrypted connection between the remote device and the company LAN, ensuring data privacy and security during remote access. Enhancing the internet speed does not create a secure connection. Firewalls are separate security measures that control network traffic and protect against unauthorized access; they don't create a secure connection.

7. The correct answer is **A**. Relocate the wireless router. Moving the router to a central location improves the signal coverage and reduces device interference and connection drops. Upgrading the bandwidth doesn't directly address the dropping connection issue. Completely disabling other devices may not be feasible in an office environment. Changing encryption enhances security, but it may not resolve the dropping connection problem directly.

8. The correct answer is **A**. A Wi-Fi analyzer helps identify sources of signal interference, such as overlapping channels or nearby devices, aiding in troubleshooting wireless connectivity issues. A Wi-Fi analyzer's primary purpose is to identify and troubleshoot connectivity issues rather than directly increasing speed. Changing the Wi-Fi password is a security measure but is not directly related to troubleshooting connectivity issues. Expanding coverage requires additional hardware or configuration changes, which are beyond the scope of a Wi-Fi analyzer's capabilities for troubleshooting.

9. The correct answer is **C**. Poor VoIP quality can occur when there is not enough available bandwidth to support voice data transmission, leading to audio quality issues. Outdated hardware is not directly linked to poor VoIP quality. A low battery will not affect poor VoIP quality.

Mock Exam

1. The correct answer is **C**. M.2 allows faster data transfer rates compared to traditional hard drives. M.2 is a form factor that is commonly used for solid-state drives (SSDs) and offers faster data transfer speeds than traditional hard drives. M.2 supports both SATA and PCIe interfaces. Graphics cards typically use the PCIe form factor. M.2 can be used as a boot device.

2. The correct answer is **A**. RAID 5 requires a minimum of three drives and distributes data and parity across multiple drives to provide fault tolerance. RAID 6 provides a higher level of fault tolerance with dual parity. RAID 0 offers increased read performance due to data striping without redundancy. RAID 5 does not require dedicated parity drives.

3. The correct answer is **B**. Secure Digital (SD) is commonly used in digital cameras. SD cards are widely adopted and offer varying capacities for storing photos and videos. CompactFlash (CF) was popular in the past, but it has been largely replaced by SD cards. Memory Stick (MS) is primarily used by Sony devices. eXtreme Digital (xD) cards are less common and are used in older Olympus and Fujifilm cameras.

4. The correct answer is **D**. ATX motherboards support dual-channel memory architecture. Dual-channel memory allows for increased memory bandwidth and improved system performance. ATX motherboards support both Intel and AMD processors. ATX motherboards typically have more expansion slots than microATX. Modern ATX motherboards use the 24-pin ATX power connector.

5. The correct answer is **A**. Secure Boot is a security feature provided by UEFI. Secure Boot ensures that only trusted operating system bootloaders and drivers are loaded during system startup. Although a BIOS password is a security feature, it is not specific to UEFI. The CMOS clear jumper is not a security feature provided by UEFI. TPM is a separate hardware component that provides secure storage and cryptographic functions (such as encryption and digital signatures) to enhance overall system security.

6. The correct answer is **B**. Enhanced audio quality and capabilities. An expansion sound card enhances the audio output of a computer by providing dedicated audio processing and additional audio ports. This results in better sound quality and the ability to support advanced audio features. An expansion sound card does not directly affect CPU performance. Cooling efficiency is related to cooling fans and heat sinks, not sound cards. An expansion sound card is not related to storage capacity.

7. The correct answer is **C**. To regulate the temperature of components. Cooling fans are used to circulate air within a computer system, dissipating heat generated by components such as the CPU, GPU, and power supply. This helps prevent overheating and ensures optimal performance and longevity of the hardware. Display resolution is unrelated to cooling fans. Wireless connectivity is achieved through other components, such as network adapters. Cooling fans do not impact sound quality.

8. The correct answer is **C**. To dissipate heat from a component. A heat sink is a passive cooling device that absorbs and disperses heat generated by computer components, such as the CPU or GPU. It consists of a metal finned structure that increases the surface area available for heat transfer. Heat sinks are not involved in audio signal amplification. Heat sinks are not designed for storage purposes. Heat sinks do not impact network performance.

9. The correct answer is **C**. To connect peripheral devices. Motherboard connector headers are used to provide connection points for various peripheral devices, such as USB ports, audio jacks, front panel buttons and LEDs, and internal connectors for storage devices. System configuration settings are typically stored in the BIOS/UEFI. CPU power is typically supplied through the CPU power connector. Display output is controlled by the graphics card or integrated graphics, not connector headers.

10. The correct answer is **C**. Multisocket motherboards are designed to support more than one CPU, allowing multiprocessing configurations. This is commonly seen in server-grade motherboards or high-end workstation systems. All other options are incorrect.

11. The correct answer is **C**. PostScript printing is a page description language that provides advanced graphics capabilities and color management. It offers precise control over color reproduction, resulting in more accurate and consistent color representation in printed documents. Printing speed is determined by the printer's hardware capabilities and other factors, not specifically by PostScript. Print resolution is primarily determined by the printer's hardware and the input image quality. Printer security features are not directly associated with PostScript printing.

12. The correct answer is **A**. Duplexing refers to the ability to print on both sides of a sheet of paper. This feature significantly reduces paper consumption and waste by utilizing both sides of the paper, making it an environmentally friendly printing option. Printing speed is not directly affected by duplexing. Print quality is determined by other factors, such as resolution and ink/toner quality. Printer durability is unrelated to the duplexing feature.

13. The correct answer is **B**. Removing all protective films and covers before powering on. When unboxing a device, it is crucial to remove any protective films or covers to ensure proper functionality and prevent damage to the device. All other options are less important. Keeping the original packaging materials may not be necessary in all cases. The instruction manual provides important information for setup and operation. Inspecting the device for any visible damage is essential before plugging it in.

14. The correct answer is **C**. Adjusting the paper size and type for printing. Printer tray settings involve configuring the paper size, orientation, and type to ensure compatibility with the printing requirements. This ensures that the printer feeds the correct paper size and type from the designated tray. Changing color settings only relates to a color printer. You might not decide to connect your printer to a network. Aligning print heads is specific to inkjet printers.

15. The correct answer is **A**. When selecting a printer paper, it is important to consider the weight and thickness that is compatible with the printer. Different printers have specific requirements, and using the appropriate paper weight and thickness ensures optimal print quality and prevents paper jams. Color and texture are subjective preferences and do not directly affect print quality. Paper brand and manufacturer may vary, but quality can be determined by considering weight and thickness. Paper price and affordability do not directly impact print quality.

16. The correct answer is **B**. Aligning the print heads to ensure precise ink placement. Inkjet calibration refers to the process of aligning the print heads in an inkjet printer, which ensures accurate ink placement and improves print quality, especially for documents with fine details or images. Ink cartridge settings usually involve ink-level monitoring and replacement. Connection settings relate to printer connectivity, not calibration. Cleaning the inkjet carriage is a separate maintenance procedure.

17. The correct answer is **B**. Controlling the movement of the printhead assembly. The inkjet carriage belt is a crucial component in inkjet printers. It is responsible for controlling the movement of the printhead assembly across the paper during the printing process. The belt is attached to the printhead assembly and ensures precise and accurate positioning of the printhead as it moves back and forth across the paper. This movement is necessary for the printhead to deposit ink droplets onto the paper, resulting in the desired image or text. The ink transfer from the cartridge to the printhead is typically managed by the ink supply system. Paper feed and alignment are controlled by separate mechanisms, such as feed rollers and paper guides. Maintaining optimal ink flow and print quality is influenced by factors such as ink formulation, printhead maintenance, and calibration, but not directly by the inkjet carriage belt.

18. The correct answer is **C**. A firewall is designed to monitor and control incoming and outgoing network traffic based on predetermined security rules. It filters network packets, allowing or denying access based on factors such as source, destination, port, and protocol. Data encryption is not a function of a firewall. Virus scanning is typically performed by antivirus software. User authentication is usually handled by separate authentication systems.

19. The correct answer is **C**. Overclocking involves running a computer component, such as a CPU or GPU, at a higher clock speed than its default or rated speed. This is done to achieve higher performance and potentially improve system responsiveness in tasks that are heavily dependent on the overclocked component's performance. Overclocking can potentially shorten the component's lifespan due to increased heat and stress. Overclocking often leads to increased power consumption. Software compatibility is not directly related to overclocking.

20. The correct answer is **D**. Among the options, 802.11ac offers the highest data transfer rates. It operates on the 5 GHz frequency band and supports multiple spatial streams, providing faster wireless speeds compared to the older 802.11a, 802.11b, and 802.11g standards. All other options offer lower data transfer rates.

21. The correct answer is **D**. NAT is commonly used in networking to allow multiple devices on a private network to share a single public IP address. It translates the private IP addresses of devices on the local network to the public IP address assigned to the router, enabling communication with devices on the internet. Encryption is not the primary purpose of NAT. DNS (Domain Name System) is responsible for translating domain names into IP addresses. DHCP (Dynamic Host Configuration Protocol) is typically used to assign IP addresses on a network.

22. The correct answer is **C**. FTP port 21 is specifically designed for file transfers between a client and a server. It allows users to upload, download, and manage files on remote servers. IMAP port 143 is used by an email client. HTTP port 80 is used for web page retrieval. SMTP port 25 is used for email transmission between mail servers.

23. The correct answer is **A**. Secure Shell (SSH) provides secure remote access to a server and facilitates secure file transfers between systems. SNMP is used for network management. POP is used for email retrieval. NTP is used for time synchronization.

24. The correct answer is **D**. Telnet is used for insecure remote command-line access to a server. It allows users to log in and execute commands on a remote system. DNS is used for translating domain names into IP addresses. HTTP is used for web page retrieval. SNMP is used for network management.

25. The correct answer is **B**. Simple Mail Transfer Protocol (SMTP) is the standard protocol for sending email messages between mail servers. It handles the transmission of email from the sender's server to the recipient's server. FTP is used for file transfers. HTTP is used for web page retrieval. POP is used for email retrieval.

26. The correct answer is **A**. DNS is responsible for translating human-readable domain names into IP addresses. It allows users to access websites and services using domain names rather than remembering IP addresses. DHCP is used to assign IP addresses to devices on a network. HTTP is used for web page retrieval. SNMP is used for network management.

27. The correct answer is **D**. Dynamic Host Configuration Protocol (DHCP) is responsible for automatically assigning IP addresses, as well as other network configuration parameters, such as subnet masks, default gateways, and DNS server addresses, to devices on a network. SNMP is used for network management. DNS is responsible for translating domain names into IP addresses. HTTP is used for web page retrieval.

28. The correct answer is **A**. GPS is a satellite-based navigation system that enables mobile devices to determine their precise geographic location. It utilizes signals from a network of satellites to triangulate the device's position on Earth. Wi-Fi connectivity does not directly provide location information. Bluetooth technology is primarily used for short-range wireless communication. NFC is used for close-range communication between devices.

29. The correct answer is **B**. Cellular location services estimate the location of a mobile device by triangulating the signal strength from nearby cellular towers. By analyzing the signal strength and timing information, the network can approximate the device's location. Wi-Fi positioning uses Wi-Fi access points for location estimation. Bluetooth proximity detection is used for identifying nearby Bluetooth devices. GPS satellite tracking provides precise location information through satellite signals.

30. The correct answer is **C**. To manage and control mobile device configurations and applications. MDM and MAM solutions allow organizations to remotely manage and control mobile devices, including device configurations, application installations, security policies, and data access. Encryption is typically implemented separately from MDM/MAM. Physical device security is not the primary purpose of MDM/MAM solutions. Remote wipe functionality is one of the security features but not the sole purpose of MDM/MAM solutions.

31. The correct answer is **B**. IMAP is commonly used for corporate email configuration on mobile devices. It allows users to access and manage email messages stored on a mail server, offering features such as syncing across devices and server-side mailbox management. POP3 is used for email retrieval but does not offer advanced synchronization features. SMTP is used for email transmission between mail servers. LDAP is used for directory services.

32. The correct answer is **C**. To verify the identity of users with an additional authentication factor. Two-factor authentication (2FA) adds an extra layer of security by requiring users to provide two different authentication factors to verify their identity. Data encryption during transmission is not the primary purpose of 2FA. Secure physical access to devices is typically achieved through other means, such as biometric authentication or physical keys. The primary purpose of 2FA is to enhance identity verification, although it can indirectly help prevent unauthorized access to corporate applications.

33. The correct answer is **C**. To delete all data on the stolen device remotely. The remote wipe feature allows the owner of a stolen mobile phone to remotely erase all data stored on the device. This helps protect sensitive information from falling into the wrong hands. Remote wipe does not physically retrieve the stolen device. Tracking the location of the device is typically handled by other features, like GPS or cellular location services. Disabling network connectivity is not the primary purpose of remote wipe, although it may be an additional security measure in some cases.

34. The correct answer is **B**. Enabling Bluetooth on a device allows it to discover, pair, and establish wireless connections with other Bluetooth-enabled devices. This enables data transfer, audio streaming, and other forms of communication between devices. Bluetooth is not directly related to wireless internet connectivity. GPS navigation is unrelated to Bluetooth. Bluetooth typically consumes additional battery power.

35. The correct answer is **A**. To enable pairing on a Bluetooth device, the user typically needs to press a specific button or combination of buttons on the device. This action puts the device into a discoverable mode, allowing it to be detected and paired with other Bluetooth devices. All other options are incorrect.

36. The correct answer is **A**. To find a device for pairing in Bluetooth, the device performs a scan to discover nearby Bluetooth devices. A Wi-Fi network is unrelated to finding a device for Bluetooth pairing. Syncing data is a separate process and not directly related to finding a device for pairing. Enabling location services is unrelated to Bluetooth pairing.

37. The correct answer is **A**. Access the device's settings and toggle the data network option. Enabling or disabling the wireless/cellular data network on a mobile device typically involves accessing the device's settings and locating the option to enable or disable data connectivity. Activation or deactivation is usually managed by the user through the device settings. Restarting the device does not directly enable or disable the data network. Updating the operating system does not control the enable/disable functionality of the data network.

38. The correct answer is **B**. GSM (Global System for Mobile Communications) and CDMA (Code Division Multiple Access) are wireless/cellular technology standards used for voice and data communication. They define the protocols and technologies used by mobile networks. 3G and 4G are generations of wireless technologies, not specific standards. Bluetooth and Wi-Fi are different types of short-range wireless technologies. LTE and WiMAX are specific wireless standards, but not commonly used for voice communication.

39. The correct answer is **C**. Share the device's internet connection with other devices. The hotspot feature on a mobile device allows the user to share their device's cellular data network connection with other devices, such as smartphones, tablets, or laptops. This enables those devices to access the internet using the mobile device's data connection. Hotspot functionality does not necessarily imply creating a secure network. Hotspot usage is not specifically related to high-speed data connectivity in remote areas. Hotspot usage is separate from automatically connecting to public Wi-Fi networks.

40. The correct answer is **C**. To improve the device's call and data connection quality. Preferred Roaming List (PRL) updates on a mobile device involve updating the list of preferred networks and their associated settings. This helps improve the device's call and data connection quality, ensuring that it connects to the most suitable network when roaming. PRL updates are not specifically related to international roaming. Network security protocols are separate from PRL updates. PRL updates do not directly optimize battery usage during roaming; that is typically handled by other power management features on the device.

41. The correct answer is **D**. Public addresses are assigned to devices that are connected to the internet. These addresses are globally unique and routable on the internet, allowing devices to communicate with each other across different networks.

42. The correct answer is **A**. USB 2.0 supports a maximum data transfer rate of 480 megabits per second (Mbps). It is commonly used for connecting various peripherals such as keyboards, mice, printers, and external storage devices to computers. 1 Gbps, 5 Gbps, and 10 Gbps all represent the data transfer rate of Gigabit Ethernet.

43. The correct answer is **C**. USB 3.0, also known as USB 3.1 Gen 1, supports a maximum data transfer rate of 5 gigabits per second (Gbps). 1 Gbps, 5 Gbps, and 10 Gbps all represent the data transfer rate of Gigabit Ethernet.

44. The correct answer is **A**. A LAN is a network that covers a limited area, usually within a building or a campus. It allows for the sharing of resources and communication between devices within that local area. A WAN is a network that covers a large geographical area, such as the internet. A PAN is a network that is used to connect personal devices in close proximity, such as Bluetooth. A MAN is the police, ambulance, or fire brigade within a city.

45. The correct answer is **B**. A WAN is a network that spans a large geographical area and connects multiple LANs. It enables communication and data transfer between different locations, such as offices in different cities or countries. A LAN is a network confined to a small geographic area. A PAN is a network that is used for connecting personal devices in proximity such as Bluetooth. A MAN is the police, ambulance, or fire brigade within a city.

46. The correct answer is **B**. Fast Ethernet, also known as 100BASE-TX, supports a maximum data transfer rate of 100 megabits per second (Mbps). It is a common networking standard used for Ethernet connections in both residential and small to medium-sized business environments. 10 Mbps represents the data transfer rate of 10BASE-T, an older Ethernet standard. 1 Gbps, represents the data transfer rate of Gigabit Ethernet (1000BASE-T). 10 Gbps represents the data transfer rate of 10 Gigabit Ethernet (10GBASE-T).

47. The correct answer is **D**. 10 Gigabit Ethernet (10GBASE-T). 10 Gigabit Ethernet supports a maximum data transfer rate of 10 gigabits per second (Gbps). It is a high-speed Ethernet standard used in enterprise networks and data centers to provide faster connectivity for demanding applications and increased network bandwidth. 10BASE-T is an old Ethernet standard that supports a maximum data transfer rate of 10 Mbps. 100BASE-TX supports a maximum data transfer rate of 100 Mbps. Gigabit Ethernet (1000BASE-T) supports a maximum data transfer rate of 1 Gbps.

48. The correct answer is **B**. The Cat 5 cable supports a maximum data transfer rate of 100 Mbps. 10 Mbps represents the data transfer rate of older Ethernet standards such as 10BASE-T. The Cat 5e cable supports a maximum data transfer rate of 1 gigabit per second (Gbps). 10 Gbps is beyond the capabilities of the Cat 5 cable and is supported by newer standards such as Cat 6 and Cat 6a.

49. The correct answer is **A**. A Class A private address range is 10.0.0.0 – 10.255.255.255 and it can only be used internally as these packets will be dropped by the routers on the internet. 179.16.0.0 – 179.30.255.255 and 179.16.0.0 – 179.30.255.255 are public IP addresses. 169.254.0.0 – 169.254.255.255 is the Automatic Private IP Addressing (APIPA), which is a feature in network protocols, such as IPv4, that allows devices to automatically assign themselves an IP address when a DHCP (Dynamic Host Configuration Protocol) server is not available.

50. The correct answer is **C**. Devices using APIPA will assign themselves an IP address from the range 169.254.0.0 - 169.254.255.255, ensuring temporary connectivity within a local network. Option A is incorrect as APIPA addresses are not globally routable. It indicates that the computer cannot obtain an IP address from DHCP. Incorrect answers – APIPA addresses are not globally routable, nor do they assign public IP addresses. APIPA is used within a single network, not for communication between different private networks.

Index

D

T

U

www.packtpub.com

Subscribe to our online digital library for full access to over 7,000 books and videos, as well as industry leading tools to help you plan your personal development and advance your career. For more information, please visit our website.

Why subscribe?

- Spend less time learning and more time coding with practical eBooks and Videos from over 4,000 industry professionals
- Improve your learning with Skill Plans built especially for you
- Get a free eBook or video every month
- Fully searchable for easy access to vital information
- Copy and paste, print, and bookmark content

At www.packtpub.com, you can also read a collection of free technical articles, sign up for a range of free newsletters, and receive exclusive discounts and offers on Packt books and eBooks.

Other Books You May Enjoy

If you enjoyed this book, you may be interested in these other books by Packt:

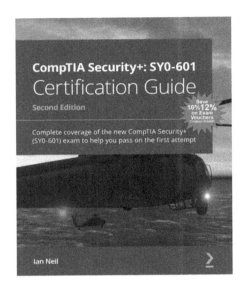

CompTIA Security+: SY0-601 Certification Guide - Second Edition

Ian Neil

ISBN: 978-1-80056-424-4

- Master cybersecurity fundamentals, from the CIA triad through to IAM
- Explore cloud security and techniques used in penetration testing
- Use different authentication methods and troubleshoot security issues
- Secure the devices and applications used by your company
- Identify and protect against various types of malware and viruses
- Protect yourself against social engineering and advanced attacks
- Understand and implement PKI concepts
- Delve into secure application development, deployment, and automation

CISA – Certified Information Systems Auditor Study Guide - Second Edition

Hemang Doshi

ISBN: 978-1-80324-815-8

- Perform an audit in accordance with globally accepted standards and frameworks
- Recognize and recommend opportunities for improvement
- Understand data analytics tools and processes
- Comprehend the effectiveness of IT governance
- Evaluate different type of frameworks
- Manage audit reporting and communication
- Evaluate evidence collection and forensics processes

Share Your Thoughts

Now you've finished *CompTIA A+ Practice Test Core 1 (220-1101)*, we'd love to hear your thoughts! Scan the QR code below to go straight to the Amazon review page for this book and share your feedback or leave a review on the site that you purchased it from.

https://packt.link/r/1837634726

Your review is important to us and the tech community and will help us make sure we're delivering excellent quality content.

Coupon Code for CompTIA A+ Exam Vouchers and Labs

Coupon Code for 13% Off on CompTIA A+ Core 1 (220-1101) Exam Vouchers

Take advantage of the **13% discount** by following the below instructions:

1. Go to https://www.testforless.store/comptia-a.

2. Click the **Buy Now** button.

3. Add the **exam voucher** to your cart.

4. From your cart, verify your credentials and product details. Then, proceed to **check out**.

5. The **13% discount** is already applied. No promo code is required.

> **The discount for the exam voucher is only available in USD. If you are purchasing from other regions, the purchase will still be made in USD. Vouchers can only be used in the countries associated with the currency in which they are purchased. View the CompTIA's Currency restrictions** (https://wsr.pearsonvue.com/vouchers/pricelist/comptia.asp) **for further clarification.**

Coupon Code for CompTIA A+ Core 1 (220-1101) Labs

Get CompTIA A+ Core 1 (220-1101) Labs for ~~$135~~ $90 and improve your skill set through practice. Access labs for 12 months from the date of purchase and get hands-on experience in a variety of exam tasks and scenarios.

Take advantage of the labs discount by following the instructions below:

1. Go to https://www.testforless.store/acore1.

2. Click the **Get Now** button.

3. Add the **lab** to your cart.

4. From your cart, verify your credentials and product details. Then, proceed to **check out**.

5. The discount is already applied. No promo code is required.